PRINCIPLES AND METHODS FOR HISTORICAL LINGUISTICS

PRINCIPLES AND METHODS FOR HISTORICAL LINGUISTICS

Robert J. Jeffers and Ilse Lehiste

The MIT Press
Cambridge, Massachusetts, and London, England

P
140
.J4

This book was set in VIP Times Roman
by Photo Graphics, Inc., and
printed and bound by The Murray Printing Company
in the United States of America

Library of Congress Cataloging in Publication Data

Jeffers, Robert J
  Principles and methods for historical linguistics.

  Includes bibliographies and index.
  1. Historical linguistics.   I. Lehiste, Ilse,
joint author.   II. Title.
P140.J4   410   78-31158
ISBN 0-262-10020-7

CONTENTS

LIST OF ABBREVIATIONS OF LANGUAGE
NAMES   vii

FOREWORD   ix

CHAPTER 1
PHONETIC CHANGE   1

CHAPTER 2
COMPARATIVE RECONSTRUCTION   17

CHAPTER 3
INTERNAL RECONSTRUCTION   37

CHAPTER 4
MORPHOLOGICAL SYSTEMS AND LINGUISTIC
CHANGE   55

CHAPTER 5
PHONOLOGICAL CHANGE   74

CHAPTER 6
EXPLANATION IN LINGUISTIC CHANGE: THE CASE
OF SOUND CHANGE   88

CHAPTER 7
SYNTACTIC CHANGE   107

CHAPTER 8
LEXICAL CHANGE   126

CHAPTER 9
LANGUAGE CONTACT AND LINGUISTIC
CHANGE   138

CHAPTER 10
THE EVIDENCE   160

GLOSSARY   173

BIBLIOGRAPHY   189

INDEX   195

LIST OF ABBREVIATIONS OF LANGUAGE NAMES

Arm.	Armenian
(Cl.) Skt.	(Classical) Sanskrit
Eng.	English
Est.	Estonian
Gmc.	Germanic
Gk.	Ancient Greek
Goth.	Gothic
Hitt.	Hittite
HE	Hiberno-English
IE	Indo-European
It.	Italian
Lat.	Latin
Liv.	Livonian
ME	Middle English
MHG	Middle High German
OCS	Old Church Slavic
OE	Old English
OHG	Old High German
OIr	Old Irish
OLat	Old Latin
OP	Old Persian
PIE	Proto-Indo-European
Skt.	Sanskrit
Sum.	Sumerian
Ved.	Vedic

FOREWORD

This book has grown out of lecture notes we developed over a number of years for an introductory course in historical linguistics taught annually in the Department of Linguistics of The Ohio State University. The course was originally designed by Lehiste and first taught in the winter quarter of 1968–69. Since the course was first offered, Lehiste has taught the course five times and Jeffers four times. Most of the material incorporated in the book has been available to students in dittoed form; we have benefited from their reactions and have tried to respond to them in preparing the version offered here. Practically all chapters have been written by both of us in turn; a version produced by one has been rewritten by the other, and the process has gone through several cycles. Readers familiar with our individual styles may be able to trace the "last hand," but basically the book is the result of close cooperation, and its merits as well as its shortcomings belong to both authors.

The history of the book explains some aspects of its form. Our course presupposes at least one introductory course in general linguistics. Because it was intended as a textbook for our course, the book does not attempt to constitute an introduction to general linguistics at the same time as it offers basic information about historical linguistics. In order to gain maximum benefit from this book, readers who come to it without any earlier exposure to linguistics are advised to read first a brief introductory general linguistics text. It should, however, be possible to understand the material without earlier formal course work in linguistics, as we have included and defined some basic terms in the glossary that belong properly to an introductory general linguistics course.

Ohio State University operates on a quarterly system. Subtracting examinations and holidays, each quarter normally comprises ten weeks of class time. The book is divided into ten chapters and provides sufficient material for fifty class hours. Suggestions for additional readings are provided at the end of each chapter. These can be used by the teacher to expand the scope of presentation for selected aspects of the topic at hand, if more class time is available. In our teaching practice, we supplement lectures with exercises, usually given as homework. We have incorporated some of our exercises in the body of the book, but since several collections of exercises are available in print, we have not included a separate appendix. The teacher can easily devise similar exercises suitable to the level and linguistic background of the class.

Another characteristic of our course that is reflected in the textbook is its relatively uncommitted nature. We do not advocate any particular linguistic philosophy; rather, we attempt to present a fair treatment of the different ways in which representatives of different linguistic schools have looked at the same historical facts. On occasion, we offer an evaluation of these different approaches, but we have endeavored to avoid any bias. We are aware that the same facts may be submitted to different interpretations; the evaluation of some of these interpretations, however, belongs at a level considerably higher than the introductory one to which we have held this book. We hope that our presentation of the basic principles involved in the study of language change through time provides the background on which an informed and intelligent evaluation of theories concerning linguistic change can ultimately be based.

In concluding, we would like to express our appreciation to our students, who have cheerfully submitted to being taught historical linguistics from the notes and materials that have finally evolved into this book. Our appreciation of the help of Marlene Deetz Payha is as great as the competence, patience, skill, and good humor she has contributed to the preparation and typing of the manuscript.

PRINCIPLES AND METHODS FOR
HISTORICAL LINGUISTICS

CHAPTER ONE
PHONETIC CHANGE

The investigation of the nature and the types of changes that affect the sounds of a language is the most highly developed area of the study of language change. The term *sound change* is used to refer, in the broadest sense, to alterations in the phonetic shape of segments and suprasegmental features that result from the operation of phonological processes. The phonetic makeup of given morphemes or words or sets of morphemes or words also may undergo change as a by-product of alterations in the grammatical patterns of a language. Sound change is used generally to refer only to those phonetic changes that affect all occurrences of a given sound or class of sounds (like the class of voiceless stops) under specifiable phonetic conditions.

It is important to distinguish between the use of the term sound change as it refers to *phonetic processes* in a historical context, on the one hand, and as it refers to *phonetic correspondences* on the other. By phonetic processes we refer to the replacement of a sound or a sequence of sounds presenting some articulatory difficulty by another sound or sequence lacking that difficulty. A phonetic correspondence can be said to exist between a sound at one point in the history of a language and the sound that is its direct descendent at any subsequent point in the history of that language. A phonetic correspondence often reflects the results of several phonetic processes that have affected a segment serially.

Although phonetic processes are synchronic phenomena, they often have diachronic consequences. The phenomenon whereby nonnasal vowels are nasalized in the environment of a following nasal consonant commonly occurs as a predictable and regular process in the world's languages. The introduction of such a process in a language where it formerly did not occur represents a sound change. When we characterize this type of dynamic phenomenon as a productive process in a descriptive grammar we use an arrow, as in V → Ṽ / _____ N. In the formal characterization of that same process as a historical event, we use a shaftless arrowhead similar to the mathematical symbols for greater than or less than, as in V > V̄ / _____ N. A formal statement of the type $x > y$ is not, however, restricted to sound changes that result from the introduction of a single new process in a language. The expression $x > y$, like the term sound change itself, is generally used to refer to any phonetic correspondence. In the history of Greek, for example, the following sound change occurs: $s > \emptyset$ / V _____ V. There is a significant body of evidence suggesting that intervocalic s first becomes h in Greek ($s > h$ / V _____ V), and that h is subsequently lost in that position ($h > \emptyset$ / V _____ V). In other words, $s > h > \emptyset$ / V _____ V can be collapsed in the statement $s > \emptyset$ / V _____ V. The sound change $s > \emptyset$ / V _____ V is the result of the introduction of at least two innovative phonetic processes in Greek, each of which represents a sound change. The statement $s > \emptyset$ / V _____ V expresses a phonetic correspondence but does not describe a phonetic process. Similarly some tokens of the Modern Greek vowel i are derived from a vowel u that occurred at a very early stage of Greek. (We shall, for the moment, term that early stage Pre-Greek.) There occurs, then, in the history of Greek a sound change $u > i$. It can be demonstrated, however, that Pre-Greek u becomes i as a result of the operation of at least two sound changes. In Ancient Greek u first becomes [y], by a process that might be termed *fronting*; it then becomes i by a process of unrounding. The sound change $u > i$ (a straightforward phonetic correspondence) is more fully elaborated by the statement $u > y > i$, where the processes that affect u as it develops toward i are identified.

Of course, the most interesting and important aspect of the study of sound change is its explanation. This issue will be considered extensively in chapter 6. In the remainder of this chapter we will be concerned simply with a presentation of many common types of sound change and of the classificatory terminology widely used in the literature to describe such changes. Certain problems presented by traditional descriptive taxonomies of sound change will also be highlighted.

CLASSIFICATION OF SOUND CHANGES

The grossest classification for distinguishing types of sound change makes reference to the range of occurrence of a given change. The fundamental distinction between *context-free* and *context-sensitive* processes is well known to students of descriptive (synchronic) linguistics. In historical linguistics the terms *unconditioned* and *conditioned* sound change are more common than context-free and context-sensitive, respectively. An unconditioned sound change may be described as one that affects the phonetic value of a sound uniformly in all environments. Unconditioned sound changes are sometimes termed *spontaneous* sound changes. A conditioned sound change affects the phonetic value of a sound in a given, statable, and usually phonetic environment. Conditioning factors are widely varied; sounds may be affected by other sounds that precede or follow, by suprasegmental factors such as stress, by the relative difficulty of producing or perceiving phonetically complex sequences of sounds, as well as by other factors.

Conditioned sound changes may be classified according to the following four categories: assimilation, dissimilation, reordering of segments, insertion or deletion of segments. This is not the only possible taxonomy of conditioned sound changes, and indeed there is some overlap in the categories delimited here. Nevertheless, this classification serves well for purposes of presentation.

ASSIMILATION

Assimilation describes any situation in which two sounds having a syntagmatic, or linear, relationship become more like one another. With reference to the phonological features phonologists use to describe speech segments, we might say that in assimilation a segment's marking (+ or −) for a given feature, such as voice, or for a group of features is changed so as to agree with the specification for that feature or complex of features in a given segment of its vicinity. Any feature or complex of features may be affected by assimilation. Examples of historical assimilation are legion in the historical grammars of languages. Consonants may assimilate to other consonants or to vowels. As a case of the former consider Latin *factum*, which has become *fatto* in Italian. (The various Romance languages—French, Spanish, Portuguese, Italian, Rumanian, and others—are descended from a language whose most stylized form is Classical Latin.) Note the assimilation of [k] to [t]. In the prehistory of Italian all clusters of stops and of nasals assimilate in this manner; for example, Latin *septem* 'seven', *somnum* 'sleep' become Italian *sette, sonno*. Consonants may take on features of adjacent vowels. *Palatalization* and *labialization*, for example, are common historical processes. The initial palatal affricates in English words like *church* (OE *ciricе*), *chide* (OE *cīden*), and *cheek* (OE *cēace*) develop from *k* (spelled *c* in Old English), which has undergone palatalization in the environment of following palatal vowels.

Stops may become continuants in the context of other continuants, commonly vowels. In the prehistory of Hindi, intervocalic stops become glides; consider the form *gata-* 'gone' in the ancient Indic language Sanskrit and *gayaa*, its descendent in Modern Hindi. Similarly, Ancient Greek voiced stops develop as fricatives in Modern Greek; compare the pronunciation of δ in Ancient Greek ᾿αδελφοϩ [ádelpʰos] and Modern Greek αδελφοϛ [aðelfos].

Assimilation may be complete or partial. The result of *complete assimilation* is a pair of identical segments. The consonant assimilations of Italian are examples of complete assimilation. It should be noted that many, perhaps most, complete assimilations are the result of a series of separate processes that have operated in the course of the progressive development of a language. In the case of It. *sonno*, for example, it is known that a form of the shape *swepnom* predates Lat. *somnum*, which itself is the source of It. *sonno*. The medial cluster of *sonno* has undergone at least two assimilatory processes in its prehistory: a partial assimilation whereby the labial stop [p] becomes the labial nasal [m] so as to agree with a following [n] with respect to the feature [nasal], and a second assimilation for point of articulation. As the result of a partial assimilation, the sound undergoing phonetic change and the conditioning sound come to share identical markings for a greater number of features. The terms complete and partial assimilation are generally used to refer to changes that affect sequences of consonants.

In many of the examples of assimilation we have considered so far, the conditioning segment follows the sound that changes. The Italian consonant assimilations and the English palatalization of velars just described are examples. A change such as this, in which a sound is altered through some form of anticipation so as to conform in any degree to a segment that follows, is termed a *regressive assimilation*. In other situations the conditioning element precedes the assimilated sound. The fronting *t* to *ch* [*č*] in Spanish words like *fecho* from earlier *feito* (< *factum*) is an example. The term *progressive assimilation* describes such changes. The Slavic languages offer a similar example of progressive assimilation.

Because of alternations that occur in all of the Slavic languages, we can be sure that the affricates *c* [ts] and *ʒ* [dz] are not original but are historically derived from the velar stops *k* and *g*. One context where such a change occurs is in the environment of certain preceding front vowels. The so-called Slavic progressive palatalization may be formulated as follows: *k, g* > *c, (d)z* / {*i̧, ĭ, ȩ̄*} ____. For example, Old Church Slavic (OCS) *ovica* 'sheep' < **ovika*, compare Skt. *avikā* 'sheep': OCS *stĭ(d)za* 'path' < *stiga*, compare Gk. *stokhos* 'line': OCS *kŭnĕ(d)zĭ, kŭnēzĭ* 'king, prince' < **kuningaz*, compare Old High German *kuning* 'king'. It is interesting to note that some tokens of *c* and *(d)z* develop as a result of a regressive assimilation, the so-called second regressive palatalization of Slavic. When followed by front vowels that are historically derived from diphthongs (*i* and *ě* [æ] < *ei* and *oi, ai*, respectively), *k* and *g* become *c* and *(d)z* in Slavic.

In all of the instances of assimilation given thus far, the conditioning segment has been immediately adjacent to the changed sound. This is not always the case, and we consequently distinguish between *adjacent assimilation* and *distant assimilation*. It often happens, for example, that vowels are fronted or backed, raised or lowered, in the context of a vowel of corresponding quality in an adjacent syllable. When the conditioning vowel follows the vowel that undergoes a change in quality, the German term *umlaut* is commonly used to describe the change. If the conditioning vowel is first in the sequence, the term *vowel harmony* is used. An example of vowel harmony for height in Irish is discussed extensively in chapter 3.

DISSIMILATION
Dissimilation describes a situation in which one sound has become *less* like another in its vicinity. Not all sequences of like sounds are as liable to dissimilation as others. Liquids, nasals, and segments that demand complex readjustments in the glottis, such as aspirated, murmured, and glottalized stops, seem particularly prone to dissimilation. Dissimilation of liquids is especially common in the world's languages. English offers examples in a number of Latin words borrowed into English; compare for example Latin *peregrinus* and *purpur* with English *pilgrim* and *purple*. Compare also French *flairer* 'to scent' with earlier *fragrare* 'to smell' in Latin. The name of the Italian city Bologna offers an example of dissimilation in a sequence of nasals. The earlier form of that place name is Bononia.

Perhaps the most well-known example of a historical dissimilation is a phenomenon in Ancient Greek and Sanskrit known as Grassmann's Law. In Greek an aspirate stop becomes a plain voiceless stop if another aspirate appears in a following syllable. Similarly in Sanskrit, a voiced aspirate (murmured) stop becomes a plain voiced stop in the context of a following voiced aspirate (murmured) stop. The results of these developments are particularly notable in reduplicated verb forms. Compare (Gk.) *tithēmi*, (Skt.) *dadhāmi* 'I place' with (Gk.) *didōmi*, (Skt.), *dadāmi* 'I gave'.

REORDERING OF SEGMENTS
It is sometimes the case that the order of segments will be reversed in specific lexical items or in a class of forms that show specific sequences of segments. The term *metathesis*

describes a situation in which the shift of order affects adjacent segments. *Spoonerism* refers to such shifts when the segments involved appear in different syllables, or more commonly, in different words. The example, "Sew her shadylip to her sheet," is attributed to the Reverend William A. Spooner, who reportedly wanted to say "Show her ladyship to her seat." Spoonerisms are generally sporadic, reflecting one-time-only errors of production. The phenomenon has little if any long-term effect and is of minimal interest in the study of linguistic change. Metathesis, on the other hand, can be sporadic or regular and often results in linguistic change.

Metathesis can be sporadic in both a linguistic and temporal sense. A certain shift of order may affect a given sequence in one or a few words, once or on occasion, in the speech of a particular individual. Most speakers of English have heard or produced a form like [æks] for [æsk] 'ask' on occasion. Sucl alterations are not, however, restricted to occasional lapses. They can and often do result in linguistic change. Some Ancient Greek dialects regularly show the metathesis *ps > sp* / # ____. Attic *Psyche* corresponds to dialectal *Spyche*.

Historical metatheses are not necessarily restricted to specific words or small classes of words. Armenian (Arm.) shows an excellent example of a completely regular metathesis. It affects all clusters of the shape consonant (C) plus liquid (L) in any position. For example Arm. *surb* 'bright' is known to be derived from an earlier form *subhro-*; compare the related Sanskrit form *subhra-* 'bright'. The Armenian metathesis affects CL clusters, even when they occur in word-initial position. Compare Skt. *bhrātar-* and Arm. *ełbayr* 'brother'. The *r* sometimes becomes *ł* in Armenian, and a prothetic, or word-initial, vowel develops regularly in words that begin with a liquid.

Metatheses are, for the most part, restricted to certain types of sequences of segments, namely clusters that include a sibilant and a stop, as well as sequences of liquids and vowels (V) or consonants. A regular metathesis of VL to LV occurs in Slavic (for example, Pre-Slavic **gordu > OCS gradŭ* 'town'). Metathesis is unquestionably used appropriately as a descriptive device in the case of this Slavic sound change. It describes a formal relationship that holds between the shapes of a set of forms at two stages in the history of a language. It describes a phonetic correspondence. As is the case with many of the types of sound change discussed in this chapter, however, all historical metatheses do not necessarily reflect the operation of a phonological process of metathesis. This Slavic development is, perhaps, a case in point. Many pho- nologists believe that historical metatheses of the type VL > LV or LV > VL reflect the end result of a sequence of events that might be characterized as follows: . . . CVLC . . . > . . . CḶC . . . > . . . CLVC . . . (Ḷ represents a syllabic liquid); the opposite processes would affect original sequences like . . . CLVC . . . The alternant pronunciations of English words like *western* as [wɛstərn ~ wɛstṛn ~ wɛstrən] apparently exemplify the operation of the very same processes that may explain histor- ical metatheses of the type noted in Slavic.

Ancient Greek offers another example of a historical cor- respondence that has been called a metathesis, but which probably reflects a more complex sequence of events. The verb *bainō* 'I go' and the noun *moira* 'fate' are derived from the forms (Pre-Greek) gʷmyō > *bamyō* > *banyō* and *morya*, respectively. These words exemplify a change whereby clus- ters of nasals or liquids plus glides are said to metathesize. There is, however, an extraordinary restriction on the meta- thesis. The shift occurs only when the vowel preceding the cluster is nonhigh and nonfront, that is, *a* or *o*. The following series of processes has been suggested to explain the apparent metathesis:

(1.1)
gʷmyō > bamyō > banyō > bańyō > baińyō > baińō > bainō

Note that this series of developments suggests a palatalization of the liquid or nasal in the environment of nonsyllabic *i* (*banyō* > *bańyō*), and the subsequent introduction of what might be termed a transition glide between a nonpalatal vowel and a following palatalized consonant (*bańyo* > *baińyō*). This would explain the restriction on the introduction of the glide in preconsonantal position, since *a* and *o* are the least palatal vowels, and a major articulatory transition is necessary. Moreover, we know from many other developments in Ancient Greek that there was indeed widespread palatalization of consonants in the environment of following nonsyllabic *i*, and that there was a subsequent loss of nonsyllabic *i* and loss of palatalization. Although the term metathesis might be considered a useful description of the relationship between the early form *banyō* and the Gk. form *bainō*, it should be noted that it does not describe the actual development (in this case, series of developments) that brought about the phonetic correspondence to which the term refers.

It should be pointed out that the term metathesis, as used in the historical linguistic literature, is not restricted to the description of changes that affect full segments. The Attic dialect of Ancient Greek, for example, is said to have been affected by a *quantitative metathesis* in the course of its prehistory. Sequences of the type $\bar{V}\breve{V}$ are replaced by $\breve{V}\bar{V}$. Consider the genitive case of certain Ancient Greek nouns with stems that end in a long vowel. The regular genitive case ending is *-os* (as in *podos*; nom. *pous* 'foot'). However, words like *basileus* 'king' have genitive case forms with a long vowel in the ending; *basileōs* comes from earlier *basilēos* (compare the archaic genitive *basilēos*, which occurs in Homer, and which does not show the quantitative metathesis).

A metathesis of resonance may also occur. Such a phenomenon affected the Germanic language, Gothic. The plural of the word *sunus* 'son' is *sunjus*. We know that *sunjus* is derived from a form **sunewes* (**sunewes* > Goth. *suniws* > *sunjus*, where *j* represents nonsyllabic *i*). After the loss of vowels in the last syllable of a word and the raising of *e* to *i* in Germanic, the sequence VR (R = resonant) is replaced by a corresponding RV sequence (*iw* > *ju*) in Gothic. Words with similar sequences are altered in a like manner. The factors responsible for changes of this type may be varied and complex. We might expect them to be related to shifts of accent that often affect syllable structure.

INSERTION OR DELETION OF SEGMENTS

We have seen that the phonetic value of segments can change
in a great variety of ways in the course of the development of
a language. It is also common for segments to be lost under
specifiable conditions, and in some instances a particular segment may be entirely eliminated from the sound system of a
language. Moreover, segments may be introduced into contexts where they did not exist previously. Such *intrusive* segments may be sounds that occur in the language, or they may
be entirely new to the sound system. Several technical terms
are used to classify the historical introduction or deletion of
sounds.

Vowel loss is commonly associated with the development
of an innovative accentual system (commonly a stress system)
or with a change in the position of accent. Loss of an initial
vowel is termed *aphesis* (or *aphaeresis*). The dialectal English
possum from *opossum* is an example. *Apocope* is the loss of
word-final vowels. The so-called mute *e* of English or French
represents an orthographic archaism attesting to the earlier
presence of word-final vowels in many of the words spelled
with a word-final vowel that is no longer pronounced. The
English word *tale* was in Early Middle English pronounced
with final *ə*, as [ta:lə]. *Syncope* refers to the loss of vowels
within a word. Old English *munecas* 'monks', for example,
becomes Middle English *munkes ~ monkes*. (The Modern
English singular *monk* is introduced on the basis of the syncopated plural form discussed in chapter 4.)

Vowels are often inserted between consonants to facilitate
pronunciation in forms that have developed articulatorily difficult consonant clusters. *Epenthesis* is the most common term
for such a phenomenon. The terms *anaptyxis* or *svarabhakti*
(Greek and Sanskrit, respectively) are likewise commonly
used to refer to the epenthesis of vowels, the quality of which
can be predicted on the basis of segments in their phonetic
environment. Latin *facilis* 'easy' and *pōculum* 'goblet' from
earlier *faclis* and *pōclum* show anaptyctic vowels whose quality is dependent on that of the vowels in following syllables.
The development of word-initial vowels is called *prothesis*. In

the earlier discussion of the historical metathesis of Armenian consonant plus liquid clusters, the introduction of a prothetic vowel before word-initial liquids was noted, as in *ełbayr* 'brother'. Spanish shows prothesis in the environment of *s* plus stop clusters. Compare *escuela* 'school' with the earlier form noted in Lat. *schola*. The term *paragoge* is generally used for the development of word-final vowels, but this is probably an uncommon sound change, possibly arising only as a result of the development of final clusters that are articulatorily difficult. Most paragogic vowels are the result of language contact, developing when words ending in a consonant are borrowed by speakers in whose native language all words end in a vowel. The following schema gives the major terms for the introduction and loss of vowels:

(1.2)

	Initial	**Medial**	**Final**
Addition	prothesis	anaptyxis epenthesis svarabhakti	(paragoge)
Loss	aphaeresis aphesis	syncope	apocope

The loss of a whole syllable in a sequence involving duplicated or nearly duplicated syllables is called *haplology*. This process has yielded Latin *nūtrīx* from earlier *nūtritrīx*, and *stīpendium* from *stipipendium*. Similarly, in English *interpretative* has become *interpretive; phonemicization* has given *phonemization*.

Of the possible ways in which consonants may be added, the most frequently attested is the development of excrescent *plosives* in clusters of nasals plus consonants. These plosives usually share point of articulation features with adjacent sounds, and their development can be explained by a change in the timing of the articulatory gesture involved in the closing of the nasal passage. By such a process Old Spanish *vendré* 'come' developed from a form like Latin *venire*, with earlier syncopation of medial *i*. In Spanish such excrescent consonants develop even in Arabic loan words, such as *Alhambra* from *al hamra*. Excrescent consonants less commonly develop in clusters that do not include a nasal. Vulgar Latin *essere*, for example, has developed into Old French *estre* (after syncope of the vowel of the second syllable), from which developed Modern French *être*.

There exist no special terms for the loss of consonants. Consonants may be lost in a variety of contexts, most commonly in complex consonant clusters; compare Middle English *answerie* 'answer' and *gospel* with earlier *andswerien* and *godspelle*. Consonants are also commonly lost in intervocalic position. The loss of intervocalic consonants is often the ultimate result of a series of processes. In most cases of intervocalic consonant loss, intermediate stages with *h* or a glide are attested or can be reconstructed.

It is commonly the case that the loss of a consonant is associated with an increase in the quantity of a preceding vowel. Such developments are termed *compensatory lengthening* and generally serve to maintain the quantitative integrity of a syllable. The spelling of the Modern English word *night* points to an earlier word final consonant cluster. In Old English *night* was pronounced [nixt]. Associated with the loss of the consonant x, we note a lengthening of the vowel *i* to *ī*. The source of the diphthong in Modern English *night* [nait] is the long vowel *ī*. Hence, the first step in the development of the word *night* from Old English to Modern English is an example of compensatory lengthening, whereby *nixt* > *nīt* > *nait*.

Compensatory lengthening often refers to a phonetic correspondence that can be shown to result from a series of phonetic processes. Consider words like Sanskrit *nīdā* 'nest'. It is known that the source of the word is the compound form *ni* 'down' + *sd* (a morphophonemic alternant of *sad*) 'sit'. The development of the root of the word from *nisd-* to *nīḍ-* results from (1) a regular voicing assimilation, *nisd-* > *nizd*; (2) a regular retroflexion of *z* after *i-*, *nizd-* > *niẓd*; (3) regular retroflexion of dental stops after retroflex sibilants, *niẓd-* > *niẓḍ-*; (4) a regular change of *z* > *y*, *niẓḍ-* > *niïḍ-*; and (5) a regular contraction of a palatal vowel and palatal glide, *niïḍ-*

> *nīḍ-*. To recapitulate: *nisd-* > *nizd-* > *niẓd-* > *niẓḍ-* > *niïḍ-*
> *nīḍ-*.

DOMAIN OF PHONETIC CHANGE

The domain of a phonetic process or a set of processes in a language is sometimes greater than the word. The loss, introduction, or alteration of a sound in the context of a transition from one word to another is termed *sandhi*. Such processes often have far-reaching historical effects, especially when conditioning elements are lost. In the prehistory of Irish, word-final segments conditioned sound changes in the initial segments of following words in syntactic phrases, such as noun phrases and verb phrases. Most final syllables were subsequently lost, obscuring the conditions on the mutation of word-initial consonants. As a result Old Irish appears to inflect words at the beginning and at the end. A more thorough discussion of the historical effects of sandhi in Irish is given in chapter 3.

CLASSIFYING UNCONDITIONED SOUND CHANGES

The classification of unconditioned sound changes is far less well developed than that of conditioned sound changes because context-free processes are, in general, less well understood than context-sensitive processes. The terminology for changes in tongue position and lip rounding in the articulation of vowels is obvious—*centralization, raising* and *lowering, fronting* and *backing, rounding*. Consonants may be similarly affected by unconditioned changes in their articulatory dimensions, that is, in their manner and point of articulation.

Frequently, unconditioned sound changes affect entire classes of sounds in a language. Such developments are called *sound shifts*. English shows the reflexes of two far-reaching sound shifts, one affecting consonants—the so-called first Germanic consonant shift, and one affecting long vowels, the so-called great English vowel shift. It is widely assumed that as a result of the first Germanic consonant shift, voiceless stops become fricatives, voiced stops become voiceless, and aspirate stops become simple voiced stops. That is to say, p, t, k > f, θ, χ; b, d, g > p, t, k; b^h, d^h, g^h > b, d, g. The great English vowel shift results in a general raising of long vowels, and the diphthongization of the high vowels, i and u. Consider the following diagrams:

(1.3)

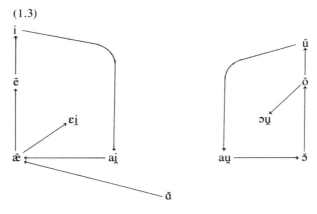

CHANGES IN PROSODIC FEATURES

Not only may phonological change affect the system of segmental sounds, but the prosodic system of a language may undergo various types of changes, which, in turn, may affect the segmental system. Each of the three prosodic features—quantity, tone, and stress—may be involved in the change. Languages may lose an original quantity opposition or develop a new one; languages may lose or acquire distinctive tone; formerly free and distinctive stress may become fixed and acquire the value of a boundary signal, or stress shift patterns may develop that acquire linguistic function. All these prosodic changes may interact with segmental changes, either resulting from a change in the segmental system or producing a change in the segmental system as a result of the change in the suprasegmental system.

The following example illustrates some possibilities. It is well known that Latin at one time possessed a quantity opposition in vowels; words like *populus* `people` and *pōpulus* `poplar` constituted minimal pairs. Developing into the various Romance languages, the parent language lost the original quantity opposition, replacing it by a system involving a larger number of vowels differing in phonetic quality. Latin started with a basic system of five vowels, which could be either long or short: *ī, i; ē, e; ā, a; ō, o*; and *ū, u*. At an intermediate stage (often referred to as Vulgar Latin), the length opposition was lost; long *ī* and *ū* continued as [i] and [u], short *i* merged with long *ē* as [e] and short *u* merged with long *ō* as [o]; short *e* became phonetic [ɛ] and short *o* developed into [ɔ]; the length distinction between *ā* and *a* disappeared, leaving a seven-vowel system without a length opposition. Individual Romance languages have undergone further developments; Italian, for example, shows diphthongs in words that, in Latin, contained short *e* and short *o* in open syllables.

(1.4)

Vowel	Latin	Italian	
ī	cĭnere	cenere	`ashes`
ē	cēra	cera	`wax`
ĕ	dĕcem	dieci	`ten`
ŭ	crŭce	croce	`cross`
ō	corōna	corona	`crown`
ŏ	bŏnu	buono	`good`

(Italian ẹ = [e], e = [ɛ], ọ = [o], o = [ɔ].)

The Italian stressed vowels in open syllables are phonetically longer than unstressed vowels. Note that the development of diphthongs from short vowels implies that the loss of the quantity opposition must have evolved by way of lengthening of short vowels rather than through a reduction of the duration of long vowels. In Latin, vowel length was independent of stress; in Italian, stress conditions the length of vowels, and vowel length may be considered a stress cue. The change in one suprasegmental feature (quantity) has brought about a restructuring of several different aspects of the phonological system.

RECOMMENDED READING

Bloomfield, L. (1933) *Language,* Holt, Rinehart and Winston, New York, chapters 20 and 21.

Sapir, E. (1921) *Language*, Harcourt, Brace and World, New York, chapter 8.

CHAPTER TWO
COMPARATIVE
RECONSTRUCTION

The comparative method is based on two underlying assumptions. The first might be called the *relatedness hypothesis*, the second the *regularity hypothesis*. The relatedness hypothesis tries to explain obvious similarities between words belonging to different languages or dialects by assuming that these languages are related. It assumes that the languages and dialects are descended from a common ancestor language or *protolanguage*. The regularity hypothesis makes it possible to reconstruct that protolanguage by assuming that sound changes are regular. It assumes that each sound of a given dialect will be changed similarly at every occurrence in like circumstances, if it is changed at all. The comparative method consists of examining words with similar meanings in languages suspected of being descended from a common protolanguage, in hopes of discovering *sound correspondences* and reconstructing the protolanguage.

ESTABLISHING SOUND CORRESPONDENCES

The procedure involves examination of sounds in a particular place in a particular morpheme. For example, the initial consonants in a set of words suspected of being *cognates* are compared with one another. Cognates are words that have descended from one and the same word of the protolanguage. Cognates usually have similarities in both form and meaning. After all sounds in analogous position have been examined and sound correspondences have been established, one may proceed to reconstruct the shape of the word in the protolanguage.

As an example, let us consider a possible reconstruction for the Indo-European word meaning 'cloud' based on a comparison of the word glossed 'cloud' in three languages we shall assume to be related: Sanskrit (Skt.) *nábhas*, Ancient Greek (Gk.) *néphos*, Old Church Slavic (OCS) *nebo*. Indo-European

(IE) is the term we use to characterize a large family of languages spoken both in ancient and modern times in Europe and Western Asia. It is the language family of which English is a member. The protolanguage from which the IE languages are derived is generally termed Proto-Indo-European (PIE). We observe a similarity in form and identity of meaning in this set of words, and hypothesize that they constitute a set of *cognates*—a set of morphemes or words in presently different languages that are derived from a single parent morpheme or word. The *sets of correspondences* for these three words are shown in (2.1). The sets of correspondences identified for the word 'cloud' in these three languages are repeated in many other morphemes of these languages.

(2.1)

Sanskrit	Classical Greek	Old Church Slavic
n	n	n
a	e	e
bh	ph	b
a	o	o
s	s	

On the basis of correspondences such as these, one attempts to establish a reconstructed form from which all sounds in the daughter languages could have been derived by plausible sound changes. The term *daughter language* is used to designate each of any number of related languages as a historical descendent or continuation of some earlier language. The cognate relationship that exists among a group of daughter languages is characterized by the term *sister language*. The reconstruction of *n* as the initial consonant is simple in this case, since all three languages show the same reflex. The term *reflex* is used here to refer to a sound occupying a specific position in a particular morpheme, which appears to be a continuation of an earlier sound occupying the same position in the same morpheme.

The reconstruction of the vowel of the first syllable is less straightforward. Sanskrit *a* corresponds to *e* in both Ancient Greek and Old Church Slavic. Since two of the daughter lan-

guages here stand against one, it appears more likely that one
of the languages has innovated and two have retained the
original state of affairs. Moreover, although we need not go
into detail here, a development from *e* to *a* in this context is
somewhat more plausible on phonetic grounds.

In the reconstruction of the medial consonant, we note that
each of the three languages offers a different reflex. However,
in each the reflex is a bilabial stop. Sanskrit and Old Church
Slavic share the feature of voice, whereas Sanskrit and Ancient Greek share a feature of aspiration. Since the segment
that appears in Sanskrit has one feature in common with each
of its sister languages, *bh* is generally reconstructed for this
set of correspondences. The choice of the symbol *bh* is of
particular interest with respect to the nature of reconstructed
forms. Although this symbol is widely used, the actual phonetic shape of the reconstructed segment is a matter of controversy among specialists in Indo-European. The symbol is
simply a formula to represent the observed correspondences.
The phonetic reality behind reconstructed forms is frequently
difficult to establish. What should be emphasized is that reconstructed forms symbolize correspondences and make no
final attempt at establishing the phonetic shape of reconstructed words. A reconstructed segment is a structural entity
of the parent phonological system.

As was the case with the first vowel of this word, for the
vowel of the second syllable, Ancient Greek and Old Church
Slavic agree in their reflexes as opposed to Sanskrit. On similar grounds, we would reconstruct *o* for the parent language.
It should be noted again, however, that the exact phonetic
quality of the reconstructed vowels is of less relevance here
than the fact that Sanskrit has restructured the phonological
system. Where the parent language has two distinct vowels,
Sanskrit has only one. The alternative would be to assume
that Sanskrit reflects the archaic situation and that Ancient
Greek and Old Church Slavic have innovated. However, if a
segment of the parent language has more than one reflex in a
given daughter language, and if the regularity hypothesis is
correct, we should expect to be able to establish the phonetic

context in which each reflex has developed. No plausible context is apparent in the data.

Sanskrit and Ancient Greek agree in showing a final consonant, *s*. There is no final consonant in the OCS word. In such a case it is best to reconstruct the word with a final consonant and to assume that *s* was lost in Old Church Slavic, at least in word-final position. The reconstructed form of the PIE word for 'cloud' would appear as **nebhos*. The asterisk is used to indicate the fact that we are dealing with a nonattested, reconstructed word rather than one that actually occurs in a language we know through written records or that is currently used by some speech community.

It can be seen, then, that for each correspondence the linguist is able to establish, one segment may be posited (at least temporarily) for the parent language. If it can be shown, however, that two or more sets of correspondences occur in contrasting environments, one is justified in reconstructing a single segment in the parent language for contrasting sets. The following example (based on Hoenigswald 1950) shows the procedure the linguist follows in reconstructing the segments of the parent phonological system.

(2.2)

	Sanskrit	Gothic	
1.	t (ásti)	t (ist)	'is'
2.	t (pitár)	d (fadar)	'father'
3.	t (bhrátar)	þ (broþar)	'brother'
4.	d (déhī)	d (digan)	'wall', 'knead'
5.	d (véda)	t (wait)	'know'
6.	dh (mádhyas)	d (midjis)	'middle'

Certain details of the relevant data from Sanskrit and Gothic have been disregarded here in order to facilitate exposition of the method. Nevertheless, example (2.2) does give a fairly accurate picture of the reconstruction of PIE dental consonants on the basis of the Indic and Germanic reflexes. Although only one pair of cognates has been given for each correspondence, it is to be understood that these cognate items are representative of correspondences that occur in a regular fashion throughout the lexicons of the two languages. The investigator may now provisionally set up six segments in the protolanguage, one representing each correspondence set. Then the investigator must consider the phonetic environments in which these correspondences occur in order to check for contrast.

Correspondence 2 occurs only in voiced surroundings and is not immediately preceded by accent in the Sanskrit forms. In contrast, correspondence 3 occurs in all those positions from which 2 is excluded. Consequently, a single segment */t/ can be set up for correspondences 2 and 3. Since correspondence 5 occurs in virtually all environments, it most probably reflects a segment of the parent language, let us say */d/ . (There are a few transparent exceptions, such as situations where Skt. *d* devoices due to a rule of voice assimilation.) Correspondence 4 occurs only when an aspirated consonant appears in the following syllable in the Skt. forms, whereas 6 can be said to occur wherever 4 does not. Thus */dh/ can be set up as the prototype for correspondences 4 and 6. Correspondence 1 is more difficult, but for the present purpose let it suffice to say (other relevant data exist) that this correspondence occurs only after *s*, whereas 2 and 3 do not. Therefore, since 1 contrasts with 2 and 3, it is reconstructible as one of the reflexes of */t/.

This very brief exercise in historical comparison has shown that, although the Sanskrit and Gothic dental consonants offer six different correspondence sets, the linguist need reconstruct only three segments for the parent phonological system. Moreover, the fact that a single segment may undergo different changes in differing phonetic environments is clearly demonstrated by the development of PIE *t* in Gothic (3 reflexes), and PIE *dh* in Sanskrit (2 reflexes).

For further practice in reconstruction, consider the cognate sets (2.3), which are based on restricted data from three Balto-Finnic languages of the Finno-Ugric family. In this reconstruction of Proto-Balto-Finnic a double consonant indicates length; vowel length in Livonian is shown by the use of the symbol : ; ä is a low front unrounded vowel; ü is a high front rounded vowel; j is nonsyllabic i; Livonian l' and r' stand for palatalized l and r; Estonian g and d are *voiceless* lenis consonants; Livonian g and d are voiced.

(2.3)

	Livonian	Finnish	Estonian	
1.	säv	savi	savi	`clay`
2.	tämm	tammi	tamm	`oak`
3.	säpp	sappi	sapp	`bile`
4.	lüm	lumi	lumi	`snow`
5.	o:da	hauta	haud	`grave`
6.	umal	humala	humal	`hops`
7.	ja:lga	jalka	jalg	`foot`
8.	ne:l'a	neljä	neli	`four`
9.	ä:rga	härkä	härg	`ox`
10.	o:r'a	harja	hari	`brush`

For cognate set 1, we must determine the quality of the first vowel, and whether the final *i* is original. All other features of the cognates agree. The front vowel of Livonian *säv* might be explained as a result of a distant assimilation (umlaut), whereby a nonfront vowel is fronted when followed by a front vowel in the following syllable. This suggested sound change, of course, assumes that the final *i* is original and that the reconstructed word is **savi*. The spontaneous development of a word-final vowel is very rare. Hence, we would independently expect the loss of final *i* in Livonian to account for the correspondence set $\emptyset : i : i$ / ____#. Note also that forms 2, 3, and 4 show this same correspondence set. Moreover, forms 2, 3, and 4 also offer support for our hypothesis about the Livonian umlaut phenomenon.

If we reconstruct **tammi* for 2, the Livonian form is explained by sound changes we have already established. The loss of word final **i* in Estonian must be explained, however. Several Estonian forms lack a final vowel where such a vowel occurs in Finnish, and sometimes in Livonian. In all forms except 1 and 4, Estonian lacks a word-final vowel where one occurs in Finnish. Forms 1 and 4 differ from all other forms in example (2.3) in that they are the only forms where the final vowel is preceded by the sequence CVC ____ . In all other forms the final vowel is preceded by either a long consonant (2, 3), a consonant cluster (7, 8, 9, 10), two syllables (6), or a vowel in the preceding syllable that is not short (the diphthong in 5). We might tentatively propose the following sound change for Estonian:

(2.4)

$$V > \emptyset / \begin{Bmatrix} CC \\ \bar{V}C \\ CVCV \end{Bmatrix} \underline{\quad} \#.$$

If we reconstruct *sappi* for 3 and *lumi* for 4, no new sound changes need be proposed.

In form 5 Finnish and Estonian agree in showing a voiceless lenis medial consonant (despite the Estonian spelling *d*), while the Livonian form has a voiced consonant. A similar correspondence is to be noted for the velar stop in 7, suggesting a sound change for Livonian, whereby voiceless stops (at least *t* and *k*) are voiced when surrounded by voiced segments. The data only offer evidence of medial voicing in the environment of sonants (S) (vowels, liquids, glides); hence, we might characterize the Livonian sound change as follows: *t, k > d, g / S* ____ *S*. The correspondence $\emptyset : h : h / \#$____ in 5 and 10 suggests the loss of initial *h* in Livonian, and the presence of *o* in Livonian *o:da* probably results from a process of monophthongization of *au*, which remains unchanged in Finnish and Estonian. Moreover, Proto-Balto-Finnic *a* must be lost in final position in Livonian in words of more than two syllables, to account for 6, Livonian *umal*.

In 7 Livonian offers a long vowel where the other two languages do not. The identical phenomenon occurs in 8, 9, and 10, presenting the general correspondence $\bar{V} : V : V$. In every case the vowel in question is followed by a liquid (*l* or *r*). A Liv. sound change of the form $V > \bar{V} /$ ____ L seems reasonable. 7 would be reconstructed as *jalka*.

In 8 and 9 we see the correspondence set $a : \ddot{a} : \emptyset /$ ____ #. We have already explained the loss of final vowels in Estonian, but the quality difference in Livonian and Finnish must be explained. Notice that all three languages agree in having front vowels in the first syllable (*e* and *ä*). A *progressive* assimilation of vowel quality suggests itself for Finnish; that is, *a* > *ä* / V (front) ＿＿. Compare the similar *regressive* assimilation (umlaut) we have proposed for Livonian.

In Estonian *neli* we see an expected vocalization of *j* after a consonant subsequent to the loss of the final vowel; that is, *j* > *i* / C ＿＿ #. Estonian *hari* (10) shows the same development. Livonian 8 and 10 are distinguished by the presence of palatalized liquids. The nonsyllabic palatal glide *j* in Finnish, which we have assumed to have become syllabic in Estonian, is surely to be reconstructed for the Proto-Balto-Finnic forms and is apparently lost in Livonian after having conditioned a palatalization of liquids, where *l*, *r* > *l'*, *r'* / ＿＿*j*; *j* > ∅ / *L'* ＿＿. Finally, the vowel of the first syllable in 10 is apparently *a*. We have already suggested a Livonian sound change whereby V > V̄ / ＿＿ L, which accounts for the length in *o:r'a*, and although the actual historical explanation is far more complex, on the basis of the data presented here we might tentatively suggest a development whereby *o:* < *a* in an open syllable.

The reconstructed Proto-Balto-Finnic forms are as follows: **savi, *tammi, *sappi, *lumi, *hauta, *humala, *jalka, *nelja, *härka, *harja*. The sound changes that have affected each language are the following:

(2.5)

Livonian
1. V (nonfront) > V (front) / ＿＿ Ci
2. i > ∅ / ＿＿ #
3. C (unvoiced) > C (voiced) / sonorant ＿＿ sonorant
4. h > ∅
5. au > o
6. a > ∅ / CVCVC ＿＿
7. r, l > r', l' / ＿＿ j
8. j > ∅ / r', l' ＿＿V
9. V > V̄ / ＿＿ $\left\{\begin{matrix} r \\ l \end{matrix}\right\}$
10. a: > o: / ＿＿ CV

Finnish

a > ä / V (front) C ____

Estonian

1. V > ∅ / $\begin{Bmatrix} CC \\ CVCVC \\ VC \end{Bmatrix}$ ____ #

2. j > i / C ____ #

Note that 1 must precede 2 and 7 must precede 8 chronologically in Livonian, and in Estonian sound change 1 must be earlier than 2.

Thus far we have given little attention to the issue of the phonetic character of the segments we have been reconstructing for the phonological systems of protolanguages. However, phonetic accuracy is becoming more possible as a result of advances in phonological theory. In order to demonstrate some possibilities for greater accuracy of phonetic detail in reconstruction, let us return to the issue of the reconstruction of the PIE consonant system. In example (2.2), a partial reconstruction of PIE stop consonants was attempted. A dental series including voiceless (*t*), voiced (*d*), and voiced aspirate (*dh*) stops was suggested. This series corresponds to that traditionally reconstructed for PIE. A similar series of labials, palatovelars, and labiovelars is traditionally reconstructed resulting in the following subsystem for PIE stops:

(2.6)

Voiceless	Voiced	Aspirates
p	? b	b^h
t	d	d^h
p	g	g^h
k^u	g^u	g^{uh}

The system quite like that given in (2.6) had been taken for granted by most scholars in Indo-European since the nineteenth century. In the 1970s, however, the phonetic character of the traditional system has been seriously called into question, as a consequence of refinements in a developing theory of phonological universals. There are several striking problems with the traditional reconstruction. The major difficulties arise from the following facts. (1) No known language with a voicing opposition has a series of voiced aspirates to the exclusion of a series of voiceless aspirates; if only one series of aspirates occurs, it is universally voiceless. (2) There is little, if any, solid evidence for the reconstruction of a voiced labial b. (Note the ? in (2.6); such a gap is unusual in the world's languages). (3) No Indo-European root of the form voiced stop + vowel + voiced stop occurs; for example, *deg* is an impossible morpheme. This constraint on the structure of morphemes seems totally unmotivated. Other problems exist, but these three will suffice for our purposes.

As a consequence of these problems several scholars have suggested revisions in the phonetic description of PIE stops. Most such revisions (see, for example, Hopper 1973) include a reanalysis of the traditional voiced stops as glottalized stops (ejectives). In languages with an ejective series, a labial (p') is commonly lacking. Moreover, sequences of the type ejective + vowel + ejective are very rare. Hence, the constraint against morphemes of the type *deg* would offer no problem if *deg* were reinterpreted as *t'ek'*. Finally, the voiced aspirate stops (sometimes called murmured stops) prove less of a problem in a system without a phonemic voicing opposition. Since voiced aspirates are characterized by a phonetic feature known as murmur in the nontraditional phonetic analysis, the three series of PIE stops would be distinguished by features of glottalization and murmur. Compare the stops in (2.6) and the following example:

(2.7)

Voiceless	Glottalized	Murmured	(= Voiced Aspirate)
p	p'	b	(= bh)
t	t'	d	(= dh)
k	k'	g	(= gh)
k^u	$k^{u'}$	g^u	(= g^uh)

The reconstruction in (2.7) remains controversial among Indo-European scholars, but it does, in any case, demonstrate the nature of modern attempts to bring a greater degree of accuracy into the reconstruction of sound systems.

THE FAMILY TREE HYPOTHESIS

As has already been noted, the comparative method assumes the relatedness of the languages to be compared. In order to characterize the nature of this relatedness, August Schleicher introduced the family tree concept in 1871. It reflects the interest of the age in the theory of evolution, and applies the hypothesis concerning the development of different species to the evolution of daughter languages from an ancestor language. The family tree hypothesis presupposes successive *splits* of fairly homogeneous earlier stages, periods of development during which changes may occur, and further splits. Through the regular recurrence of such a series of events, language families proliferate. It is assumed that after an ancestor language has split into two or more daughter languages, the speakers of the daughter languages go their separate ways, linguistically and often physically; no further linguistic contact takes place between the speakers of daughter languages. As examples a portion of the Uralic family tree and a restricted version of the IE family tree are presented in figures 2.1 and 2.2.

In the reconstruction of the history of families of languages, it is important to have a method for establishing that one language has split into two or more daughter languages. In general, language split is based on the notion of *phonological restructuring*. The sound system of a language is restructured when the system of phonological contrasts is altered in such a way that old contrasts are lost, new ones are introduced, or when the elements of the system are simply realigned. If one of two dialects of a language undergoes a development or a series of developments that restructures its phonological system, it can be said that the original language has split into two languages. In such a situation the change is irreversible, and a phonological system is established that is both innovative with respect to that of the parent language and distinct from those of the cognate languages.

In Old Indic, for example, length was clearly distinctive in high vowels. This distinction was lost in Bengali, however, as

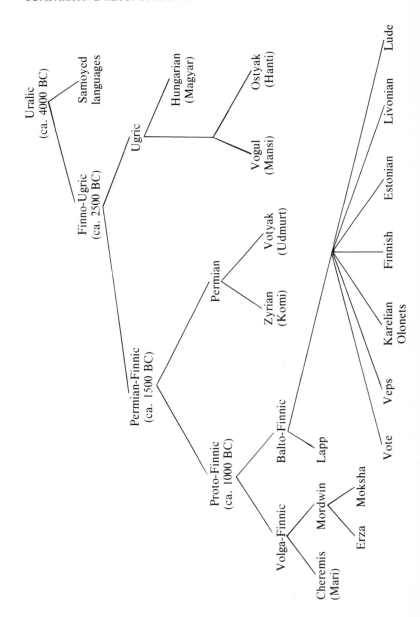

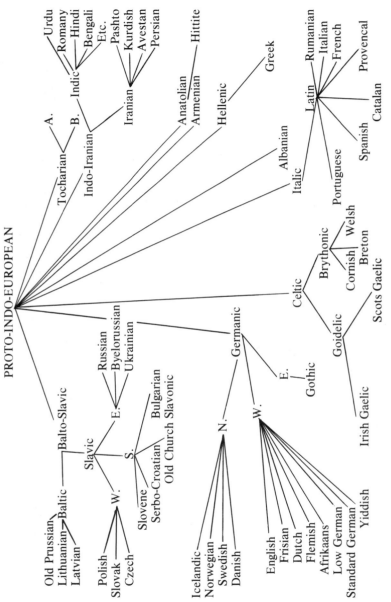

Figure 2.2 A partial family tree of the Indo-European languages

the following data show. Hindi represents the original situation as retained in a modern Indic language.

(2.8)

Bengali	Hindi	
jíb	jībh	'tongue'
din	din	'day'
dur	dūr	'distant'
šona	sun-	'hear'

That Bengali and Hindi reflect a split in the history of the Indic languages can be presumed on the basis of this restructuring (and others) in the Bengali phonological system.

A development in the consonant system of Old Irish gives another example of a similar type. The aspirates and voiced stops of Indo-European fall together in Early Celtic, eliminating a contrast in Old Irish (OIr) where there had existed one in Proto-Indo-European, and where one remains in many of its sister IE languages such as Ancient Greek, as shown by the following cognates:

(2.9)

PIE	Irish	Greek	
*g	gein	genos	'birth'
*gʰ	gēis	khēn	'swan'
*d	deich	deka	'ten'
*dʰ	dorus	tyra	'door'
*b	toib	[Lat. tibia 'shin bone']*	'side'
*bʰ	berid	pherō	'carry'

*No cognate occurs in Ancient Greek.

As was the case in Bengali, the Irish innovation is indeed an instance of irreversible change. The speaker of Irish has no way of knowing which voiced stops derive from aspirates and which do not. Moreover, since there is nothing in the phonetic makeup of the words involved that would indicate the earlier situation, even a hypothetical change of the following type would have to be based on phonetic or other factors present in Irish:

(2.10)

b, d, g $<$ b, d, g
bh, dh, gh

Because a newly restructured phonological system develops independently of its origins, the establishment of language split is based on such restructuring.

A particular sound change can, of course, be reflected in more than one related language. The fact that several languages may share particular changes implies the existence of genetic subgrouping within a language family. Such subgrouping is expected if language families do indeed reflect a series of successive splits as Schleicher suggested. Genetic relationship between some subset of the daughter languages of a larger family is defined in terms of the family tree hypothesis and is established by means of the comparative method.

Assuming three daughter languages A, B, and C, B and C can be said to be more closely related than either to A if a phonological system can be reconstructed from which B and C can be derived but which is different from that of Proto-ABC. In such a case an intermediate node may be established in the family tree as follows:

(2.11)

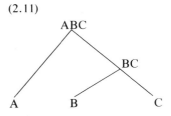

The developments that differentiate the synchronic system of Proto-BC from the synchronic system of ABC are said to be the *shared* (or *common*) *innovations* characterizing the period of common development for BC.

In (2.12) cognates from two more languages have been added to the data given for Hindi and Bengali in the foregoing discussion of language split.

(2.12)

Oriya	Assamese	Bengali	Hindi
jibhɔ	zibha	jib	jīb
dinɔ	din	din	din
durɔ	dur	dur	dūr
sun-	xun	šona	sun-

On the basis of all four languages, we would reconstruct four high vowels, *i, ī, u, ū*. However, if Hindi is disregarded, a phonological system can be reconstructed for the other three languages with only two high vowels, *i* and *u*. These three languages show a shared innovation in the merger of long and short high vowels. On the basis of this phenomenon (and certain other relevant information), these three languages are considered a subgroup in the Indic family tree, sharing a common intermediate ancestor, Proto-Oriya-Assamese-Bengali, or Proto-Eastern-Indic.

(2.13)

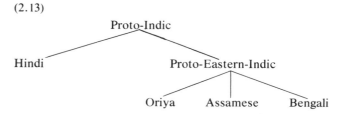

WAVE THEORY

There is a major competitor to the family tree theory of language development called the *wave theory*. Expounded first by Johannes Schmidt in 1872, the wave theory purports that linguistic innovations spread from one language or dialect through contact on the part of speakers of neighboring languages or dialects, and proponents of the theory demonstrate that languages often share innovations that cannot be attributed to a common ancestor. Two languages A and B might, for example, show reflexes of identical sound changes. A, however, might also show the reflexes of another change that is specific to language A and that must have preceded the development that is identical to the one in B. A change common to more than one language (be they related or not) that is not due to inheritance from a common ancestor is termed a *parallel development*.

Many well-known innovations can be shown to result from a wavelike diffusion from one language or dialect to another. Umlaut in the Germanic languages, for example, appears not to reflect a Proto-Germanic innovation, but seems to have spread through the Gmc. dialects after the period of differentiation. The earliest attested Germanic language, Gothic, does not exhibit umlaut. The process is found in both North Germanic and West Germanic languages; a wavelike spread of the innovation is suggested by the fact that dialects spoken in the south of Germany show many nonumlauted forms compared to dialects spoken in the north of Germany.

Although the family tree theory and the wave theory have been treated by some as opposing theories, there seems to be no reason to believe that they are mutually exclusive hypotheses about language development. Many changes can be reconstructed for Proto-Germanic and are reflected in all Germanic languages—for example, the merger of PIE $\breve{a}$ and $\breve{o}$ as a—but others, such as *umlaut*, have spread throughout the family. It is clear that these two hypotheses are complementary and that care must be taken to differentiate between changes that reflect genetic relationship and those that reflect diffusion when languages are being compared for purposes of historical inference.

DISTINGUISHING BORROWED WORDS

The borrowing of words from one language to another should not create great difficulty for comparative reconstruction if the borrowed item has been introduced from some totally unrelated language. In such a case, there probably will not be cognates in the related languages, and the borrowed form will not figure in the sets of correspondences. However, when a word is borrowed from a related language it is more than likely that there will be cognates, and it is this type of borrowing situation that might offer genuine problems to the comparativist.

Since individual sound changes are generally restricted to a specific period in the history of a language, an item borrowed into a language after a particular sound change has ceased to operate cannot be expected to show the effects of that sound change. It is by virtue of this phenomenon that the linguist can determine which items are indeed borrowed. If a form does not fit (in all of its details) into the scheme of sound correspondences that has been set up on the basis of significant numbers of items, it may be considered suspect. Consider the following example of a situation wherein a word has been borrowed from a sister language.

The Slavic form *gosĭ* (Russian *gus'* 'goose') is clearly an Indo-European word. However, the initial consonant *g* is unexpected in Slavic. There are cognates in Latin (*anser* < **hanser*), Sanskrit (*hamsa-*), Gk. (*khēn*), and Gmc. (**gan*, the reconstructed ancestor of forms such as English *goose*, German *gans*, Old Norse *gás*). On the basis of the Latin, Sanskrit, Greek, and Germanic cognates, PIE *$*\acute{g}^hans$* is reconstructible. Gmc. *g*, Lat. *h*, Skt. *h* and Gk. *kh* correspond regularly in initial position, all being derived from PIE *$*\acute{g}^h$*. Slavic *g*, however, does not reflect PIE *$\acute{g}^h$*. The expected Slavic reflex is *z*, as can be noted in cognate sets such as: Goth. *-wigan*, Lat. *veho*, Skt. *vah-*, Gk. *okhos*, Slavic *vezō* 'draw'; Lat. *hiems*, Skt. *hemanta-*, Gk. *kheima*, Slavic *zima*, 'winter'; Lat. *humus*, Gk. *khamai-*; Russian *zeml'a* 'earth, land'; *gosĭ* then cannot represent the regular development of *$*\acute{g}^hans$* in Slavic, and is generally assumed to reflect a borrowing from one of the neighboring Gmc. dialects.

In the case of Slavic *gosĭ*, the deviant word had been borrowed from a sister language (Germanic). It is also possible for a word to be introduced, or rather reintroduced, into a daughter language from the language of its origin or some dialect very closely related to that language. Such a situation often develops under the influence of a strong literary tradition. Two examples from Modern Hindi exemplify this situation.

At some time between the Old Indic period (Sanskrit) and the development of Modern Hindi, single intervocalic obstruents were either lost or became glides. (Skt. *bhrātar* > Hindi *bhāī* 'brother'; Skt. *caturtha* > Hindi *cautha* 'four'). An intervocalic obstruent is retained, however, in the Hindi word *rājā* 'king'. It is a common word in Hindi's ancestor Sanskrit, and there are a number of cognates in other Indo-European languages, such as Latin *rēx*. Its occurrence in Hindi can only be explained as a reintroduction through the influence of archaic literary Sanskrit at a period after the loss of intervocalic obstruents ceased to be operative.

The Hindi word *nām* is similarly deviant. A form *nāman-* occurs in Sanskrit, becoming *nām* in Middle Indic. Hindi shows a regular development of final -V*m* as $\bar{V}\tilde{w}$; for example, Skt. *grāma* 'village' > Mid. Indic *gām* > Hindi *gāw̃*. Most of the dialects closely related to Hindi show both *gāw̃* and *nāw̃*. The occurrence of *nām* in Hindi must then represent another situation in which the contemporary language has borrowed from a language representing an earlier stage in its own history.

RECOMMENDED READING

Bloomfield, L. (1922) *Language*, New York: Holt, Rinehart and Winston, chapter 18.

Haas, M. R. (1966) "Historical Linguistics and Genetic Relationship," in *Current Trends in Linguistics*, vol. 3, Mouton, The Hague, pp. 113–153.

Hall, R. A. (1950) "The Reconstruction of Proto-Romance," *Language* 26, 6–27.

Hockett, C. F. (1948) "Implications of Bloomfield's Algonquian Studies," *Language* 24, 117–31.

Hoenigswald, H. (1963) "Criteria for Sub-grouping Languages," in H. Birnbaum and J. Puhvel, eds., *Ancient Indo-European Dialects*, University of California Press, Los Angeles, California.

Hoenigswald, H. (1950) "The Principal Step in Comparative Grammar," *Language* 26, 357–364.

Hopper, P. J. (1973) ''Glottalized and Murmured Occlusives in Indo-European,'' *Glossa* 7.2, 141–166.

Meillet, A. (1970) *Le méthode comparative en linguistique historique*, H. Champion, Paris.

CHAPTER THREE
INTERNAL RECONSTRUCTION

Internal reconstruction has been defined as "a procedure for inferring part of the history of a language from material available for a synchronic description of the language, and from that alone" (Chafe 1959). The most straightforward form of internal reconstruction can be compared with the comparative method since it too involves the comparison of cognate forms. The procedure used in comparative reconstruction is based on the observation and the categorization of the differences to be noted in the various forms of a given morpheme as it occurs in the separate, but related, languages under analysis. In internal reconstruction, the linguist considers the various forms of a given morpheme in the single language under investigation. The paradigm, with its morphologically related but morphophonemically distinct alternants, is the starting point for one kind of internal reconstruction.

RECONSTRUCTING CONDITIONED SOUND CHANGES

Just as the comparative method assumes that different forms of related morphemes have a unique origin and that language-specific changes explain extant divergences, the method of internal reconstruction assumes that paradigmatic allomorphy is not original and that it reflects the results of one or more historical developments, usually conditioned sound changes. Hence, the historical linguist, through internal analysis, attempts to reconstruct not only the earliest shape of linguistic forms but also the specific changes responsible for synchronic alternations.

Examples of circumstances under which internal reconstruction can be applied are commonplace, especially in languages with extensive derivational and/or inflectional morphology. In German, for example, there are certain words in which an alternation between voiced and voiceless stops in various nominal case forms is observed. Although spelled with a '*d*', the word *Bund* [bunt] 'alliance' is pronounced identically with *bunt* 'gay-colored'. In inflected forms, the final [t] of *Bund* alternates with [d], whereas the [t] of *bunt* remains voiceless in all situations. In fact, corresponding paradigmatic alternations occur for all pairs of voiced and voiceless obstruents in German. The voiceless alternant appears in the paradigm of words like *Bund* only in absolute final position. On the basis of these facts, the historical linguist might assume that, at an earlier stage in the history of German, stems like *Bund* had only one phonetic shape, that with a final voiced segment. It is possible, then, to reconstruct a historical change of *d* to *t* in final position, or more generally: Obstruent (voiced) > Obstruent (unvoiced) / _____ #. A conditioned sound change has been reconstructed as part of the prehistory of German in order to explain a synchronic alternation.

The point should be stressed that, in German, voiced obstruents are sounds of limited distribution: they never occur in word-final position, where only voiceless obstruents may appear. Such limitations in distribution serve as hints that a sound change may have taken place.

Another example of a similar type is provided by Ancient Greek. In Ancient Greek there are no final stops. Stops alternate with zero in inflectional paradigms. Consider some examples: *legon* 'speaking' (nom./acc. sg. ntr.) – *legontos* (gen. sg.); *meli* 'honey' (nom. acc. sg. ntr.) – *melitos* (gen. sg.); *pais* < **paid-s* 'boy' (nom. masc. sg.) – *paidos* (gen. sg.) – *pai* (voc. sg.); *gunaikos* 'woman' (gen. sg. fem.) – *gunai* (voc. sg.). In the nominative or accusative singular of neuter nouns and in the vocative singular of all nouns there is no overt case marker in Greek. Moreover, it is clear that the genitive case ending for nouns is *-os* from classes of words like *pur* 'fire' (nom. sg. masc.) – *puros* (gen. sg.) and *pater* 'father' (nom. sg. masc.) – *patros* (Homeric), *pateros* (gen. sg.). Hence, the *t* of *legontos* and *melitos*, the *d* of *paidos*, and the *k* of *gunaikos* must be associated with the stems of these words. The historical explanation for the absence of the stem-final stops in the nominative/accusative and vocative case forms is that stops were lost in final position as the result of regular phonetic change. Again, it is possible to reconstruct a conditioned

sound change on the basis of a conditioned alternation in a
synchronic system.

In the two examples just discussed, the internal reconstruction of conditioned sound changes was uncomplicated because
no developments subsequent to those having produced the
alternations had intervened to obscure the results of the
changes under which these alternations were introduced. In
both the German and Ancient Greek cases the relevant alternations are entirely automatic in the synchronic systems, faithfully reflecting the results of a single regular sound change; no
final voiced obstruents occur in German: no final stops occur
in Ancient Greek. More commonly, the facts are not so simple.
The cumulative effect of multiple sound changes often com-
plicates the synchronic system in such a way that apparently
conflicting data present themselves to the linguist attempting
internal reconstruction. Consider the following situation occurring in several Ancient Greek dialects, discussed in Chafe
(1959).

In Ancient Greek there is a widespread alternation between
s and $\emptyset$. For example, in most dialects the genitive singular
for the word 'race' is *geneos*, whereas the dative plural is
genessi. It has already been pointed out that the genitive
singular ending in Ancient Greek is *-os*; the dative plural ending is *-si* (Compare *phulak-* 'guard' and *phulaksi* (dat. pl.)).
Hence, the alternation *gene-* / *genes-* suggests a prehistoric
sound change by which s was lost under some specifiable
conditions. Since those morphemes having an $s/\emptyset$ alternation
show the loss of s solely in intervocalic position, it can be
tentatively assumed that the sound change was of the form s
$> \emptyset$ / V _____ V. However, such an explanation seems to
conflict with certain other facts about the language. Although
the suggested sound change accounts for paradigms with an
$s/\emptyset$ alternation, intervocalic s does, indeed, occur in Ancient
Greek. In several dialects there are many words like *ambrosia*
'elixir of life' that do not belong to the paradigm class characterized by the $s/\emptyset$ alternation and that do occur with an
intervocalic s. Yet, despite the fact that the occurrence of
words like *ambrosia* appears to invalidate our hypothesis

about the conditioned loss of *s*, such is not necessarily the case. If it can be shown that an intervocalic *s* in Ancient Greek has been reintroduced by a development postdating the one that eliminated intervocalic *s* in words like *geneos*, the linguist will not only have recovered the detail of certain sound changes that took place in the prehistory of Greek, he will also have established the relative chronology of these developments.

In the case of *ambrosia,* the root *bros*- occurs with a *t* in place of *s* in paradigmatically related words like *ambrotos* 'immortal'. This alternation, *t/s*, is represented in a substantial class of words, as in *ploutos* 'wealth' and *plousios* 'wealthy'. In every such case, the alternant with final *s* is followed by *i*. The *t/s* alternation is synchronically automatic and can be assumed to reflect the historical development $t > s /$ ____ *i*. If all *s* historically derived from *t* are restored, as in **ambrotia*, words like *ambrosia* no longer confound the hypothesis about the loss of *s* that we have suggested. On the basis of internal evidence alone, then, we can assume an intervocalic loss of *s* in Greek, which was fully complete before a separate development (in many dialects) reintroduced intervocalic *s* in a limited context.

For all of the paradigmatic alternations we have considered thus far in this chapter, the conditions under which the alternations were produced are readily recoverable. This is because in each case the segments that conditioned the relevant change had themselves remained unaffected by subsequent changes. It is often the case, however, that segments that at one point in the history of a language functioned to condition sound change are themselves affected by later developments. Even so, in such cases it is usually possible to infer from the nature of the change itself the type of sound that has conditioned such a change.

LIMITATIONS OF INTERNAL RECONSTRUCTION

Classical Sanskrit (Skt.), for instance, offers a paradigmatic alternation between velar stops and palatal affricates—for example, *vāk* 'voice' (nom. sg. masc.), *vāci* (loc. sg.), *vācas* (nom. pl.). Although the alternation *k*/*c*[tš] is plausible before the palatal vowel *i*, it is clear that the nonhigh, nonfront vowel *a* could not have conditioned a change in the preceding consonant from nonpalatal to palatal. Moreover, there are many occurrences of the sequence *k*+*a* in Sanskrit (as in *kas* 'who'), where the velar stop is apparently unaffected by a following *a*. On the basis of this and other similar alternations, it is not unreasonable to assume that the *a* of the suffix *-as* is not original, and that in some earlier form of Sanskrit a more palatal vowel, which has since fallen together with *a*, occurred in its place. The reader may recall at this point that in the preceding chapter it was shown by comparison with cognate languages that the vowels *a* and *e* did, indeed, merge in Sanskrit. Even without the powerful mechanics of the comparative method, however, an internal analysis of a single type of paradigmatic alternation has permitted the reconstruction of the split of *k* into *k*/*c*, and has also suggested the basic form of a later change—the merger of some front vowel other than *i* with *a*. *Split* is the technical term used to refer to the replacement of a single segment by two or more segments in different phonetic contexts; the corresponding term, *merger*, describes a situation wherein two or more segments are replaced by a single segment. *Coalescence* is often used as a synonym for merger.

The phenomenon of merger points up the most serious limitation of internal reconstruction, which is the necessity for there to be some evidence of a change remaining in the synchronic system for the given change to be recoverable. As we have seen, the recovery of splits is generally facilitated by the presence of paradigmatic alternations in the analyzed language. However, in cases of *absolute merger*—the total loss of a phonological distinction—such residual evidence is often lacking. In fact, absolute merger is entirely unrecoverable through internal analysis, unless one of the merged segments itself functioned to condition a change that preceded the merger. This situation obtains in the case of the Skt. merger of *e* and *a*. The merger is unconditioned, but the earlier existence of *e* is indicated by its effect on preceding velar stops. Yet, even in this case, our internal reconstruction is limited to those tokens of prehistoric *e* that happened to follow a velar stop. Although it might well be assumed that the vowel *e* must have occurred in other environments, the specifics of its occurrence cannot be determined through internal reconstruction, except for this limited context: to establish, for example, that the first vowel of Skt. *nabhas* 'cloud' was historically *e* (PIE *nebhos), comparative evidence is necessary.

Germanic offers an example of a situation in which a prehistoric merger is totally unrecoverable by internal methods. Four vowels—*i, e, u, a*—are reconstructed for Proto-Germanic (PGmc.), which is the parent language of English, German, Scandinavian, the extinct Gothic, and several other northern European languages. On the basis of evidence from languages related to Germanic, we know that late Proto-Indo-European, the language from which Gmc. is derived, had five short vowels, *i, e, u, o, a*. At a very early stage in its history, Gmc. lost the distinction between *o* and *a*. The merger was unconditional, and there is no trace of evidence in Gmc. that the short vowel *a* of that language reflects two earlier and phonologically distinct segments. Hence, through internal analysis alone, historical linguists cannot fully recover the prehistoric vowel system from which Gmc. short vowels are derived, nor can we determine all those sound changes which have given the extant systems.

Even in cases where the synchronic system offers evidence of a prehistoric merger, as in the case of Skt. *a*, it is often difficult to establish the prehistoric phonetic situation in anything more than the broadest terms. Through internal analysis it can be confidently assumed that Skt. *a* has replaced at least one palatal vowel; but synchronic evidence does not enlighten the linguist with respect to the articulatory height of such a vowel (other than that it is not *i*, since *i* continues to occur in Sanskrit in all positions), nor does it show that only one front vowel is involved in the merger. However, in cases of *partial mergers* recoverable by internal analysis, the reconstruction of phonetic detail is often more straightforward. Partial merger is the loss of one or more phonological distinctions in some specifiable phonetic environment.

To illustrate this type of internal reconstruction based on the analysis of synchronic alternations, we discuss a very instructive set of data from Old Irish. The following is the singular paradigm for the OIr word 'man':

(3.1)

nom.	fer	[f'er]
gen.	fir	[f'ir']
dat.	fiur	[f'irᵘ]
acc.	fer	[f'er]

Several interesting differences are to be noted in the various case forms of this monosyllabic word. Whereas the nominative and accusative show a vowel *e*, the genitive and dative have *i*. Moreover, the final consonant is either palatalized (in the genitive), labialized (in the dative), or neutral (in the nominative/accusative). (The form *fer*, of course, represents a class of words with similar alternations.)

Just as a vowel can serve to condition change in a preceding consonant, it can also condition changes in the quality of the vowel in a preceding or following syllable. The alternations in the inflectional form of OIr *fer* might then reflect sound changes conditioned by following vowels that have been lost by subsequent changes. If the presence of these lost vowels is tentatively accepted for prehistoric Irish, much can be recovered concerning the phonetic features of these vowels on the basis of the nature of the alternations in the extant language. We might assume, for example, that the high vowels of the genitive and dative case forms suggest lost high vowels in the following syllable, whereas the midvowel of the nom./ acc. form would suggest the reconstruction of a corresponding nonhigh vowel in the hypothesized endings of these words. Furthermore, a final palatalized consonant in the genitive and a final labialized consonant in the dative imply that the lost high vowels of these two forms are palatal (like *i*) and labial (like *u*), respectively. (As synchronic evidence for the palatal character of the lost vowel of the genitive, note the automatic palatalization of a consonant, here *f*, before a palatal vowel; compare *fáith* [fɑθ'] 'prophet' having no palatalization of initial *f*.)

Our reconstruction need not stop at this point, however. Consider the following noun + adjective paradigm from Old Irish:

(3.2)

nom. sg.	fer gel	[f'er g'el]	'a bright man'
gen. sg.	fir gil	[f'ir' ɣ'il']	
dat. sg.	fiur giul	[f'irᵁ ɣ'ilᵁ]	
acc. sg.	fer ngel	[f'er ŋ'el]	

The adjective *gel* 'bright' shows vowel and final consonant alternations identical to those detailed for the noun *fer*. Apparently, conditioning factors similar or identical to those affecting nouns like *fer* were operative in the case of certain adjectives as well. (Just as this type of alternation is characteristic of a particular class of nouns in Old Irish, it is limited to a subset of adjectives.) Changes in the phonetic shape of the adjective *gel* are not, however, restricted to those affecting its head noun. The initial consonant of the adjective has three forms: velar stop, velar fricative, velar nasal. Corresponding alternations of the type $b \sim \beta \sim m$ and $d \sim \eth \sim n$ also occur.

If we continue to proceed on the assumption that it should be possible to explain synchronic alternations in terms of historical changes, these initial consonant mutations (as they are termed in Irish grammars) demand a historical treatment. It should be noted that initial consonant mutations are largely restricted to noninitial words in phrases that show close grammatical association, such as *article + noun* or *noun + adjective*. This factor suggests we are dealing with a process that must have its origin in a sandhi phenomenon, which is to say, in a situation wherein the domain of phonetic change is more extensive than the individual word. If this is so, it may be possible to go further in our recovery of lost finals by means of an analysis of the nature of the synchronic alternations to be noted in the initials with which these lost word-final segments were once in close syntagmatic contact.

Although the phonetic factors involved are often quite complex, it would not be incorrect for our purposes (though perhaps oversimplified as a general principle) to state that plosives are commonly "weakened" in intervocalic position. The effect of this "weakening" varies in different situations, but such a change frequently takes the form of spirantization for both voiced and voiceless stops. (It would be informative to point out here that voiceless initial stops in Old Irish become fricatives in just those contexts where $b, d, g > \beta, \delta, \gamma$, as in (nom.) *fer cain* [f' er can'] 'good man', but (gen.) *fir chain* [f' ir' xan'].) This commonplace change from stop to fricative in intervocalic position suggests a historical explanation for the alternation exemplified in the initial of *gel* in (3.2).

If the high vowels tentatively reconstructed for the genitive and dative forms of the word *fer* are indeed word-final, an appropriate intervocalic context for a sound change of the form stop > fricative / V _____ V would be present in prehistoric Irish, and would explain the continuant γ in the genitive and dative of the adjective *gel*. On the other hand, the maintenance of an initial stop on the nominative singular of the adjective might suggest a final consonant in the prehistoric nominative of preceding *fer*.

Up to this point the surface identity in the shape of the nominative and accusative forms of *fer* has been maintained in our reconstruction. In both, a nonhigh, nonpalatal vowel has been reconstructed. However, if the shape of the following adjective is considered, and if the assumption that unattested finals affected following initials is correct, it becomes clear that the nominative and accusative of the noun were at one time distinguished. It is reasonable to suggest that the initial alternations such as $g \sim \eta$ in the adjective reflect the influence of an earlier word-final nasal in the accusative of the preceding noun. Coincidentally, we might infer that the final consonant suggested for the prehistoric nominative would have been nonnasal.

We are fortunate in the case of Old Irish to have many cognate languages available for comparison. Consequently, our picture of the prehistoric form of that language is far more complete than any we can reconstruct solely through the methods of internal analysis. It is, however, an interesting and instructive exercise to exhibit the potential and the limitations of internal reconstruction in a situation where the reconstruction can be verified. In the case of OIr noun inflection, a striking, yet limited degree of accuracy is attainable for the class of nouns that we have considered here. Compare the endings recovered through internal reconstruction to those known to be correct for prehistoric Irish on the basis of comparison with other Celtic and Indo-European (IE) languages, as shown in (3.3).

(3.3)

Recoverable by internal reconstruction		Actual reconstruction
(V)owel	+ (C)onsonant	
nom. $\begin{pmatrix} -\text{high} \\ -\text{palatal} \end{pmatrix}$	$(-\text{nasal})$	$-\text{os}$
V		
gen. $\begin{pmatrix} +\text{high} \\ +\text{palatal} \\ -\text{labial} \end{pmatrix}$	$(\text{e.g., } -\text{i})$	$-\bar{\text{i}}$
V		
dat. $\begin{pmatrix} +\text{high} \\ -\text{palatal} \\ +\text{labial} \end{pmatrix}$	$(\text{e.g., } -\text{u})$	$-\bar{\text{u}}$
V	+ C	
acc. $\begin{pmatrix} -\text{high} \\ -\text{palatal} \end{pmatrix}$	$(+\text{nasal})$	$-\text{om}$

STRUCTURAL INCONSISTENCY AND INTERNAL RECONSTRUCTION

As has been noted many times thus far, only those linguistic changes that have left behind some traces can be reconstructed by the methods of internal reconstruction. Such traces of change are, however, not restricted to cases of paradigm allomorphy; they may involve the occurrence of structural inconsistencies of various types in synchronic systems. The

presence in a language of any of the following structural phenomena might suggest linguistic change at an earlier stage in
the history of that language: (1) disproportionate figures in the
statistical occurrence of linguistic constructs, (2) asymmetry
in the structural patterns of a language (for example, unmotivated gaps in the phonemic inventory), (3) anomalies with
respect to the canonical shape of linguistic forms.

In the case of (1) or (2) above, it is easy to speculate about
the fact of change, but it is extremely difficult to establish the
details or circumstances of a change with this kind of evidence.
In Modern Greek, for example, *i* is by far the most prepon-
derant vowel. Because we are fortunate to have a long history
of written records for Greek, we know that Modern Greek *i*
derives from nine different phonemic sources that have
merged unconditionally. If our knowledge of Modern Greek
were isolated, and if Modern Greek did not use archaic spell-
ings, the extraordinary statistical preponderance of *i* within
Greek would be the only hint that the original state of affairs
might have been different. Of course, nothing in the modern
language suggests the details and the magnitude of that difference.

The use of structural patterns as evidence that a linguistic
change might have taken place (2) is based on the well-estab-
lished assumption that languages will, in general, tend to conform to certain principles. It is widely held, for example, that
sound systems will universally tend to be symmetrical. Thus,
if a language has a full set of voiced stops but lacks only one
of the corresponding voiceless stops, it would be reasonable
to assume that the missing voiceless stop had been eliminated
through the operation of a sound change. In Old Irish the stops
g, d, b, k, t occur. The stop *p* occurs only in a few obviously
and lately borrowed loanwords from Latin; it is uniformly
lacking in the native vocabulary. The inference that *p* was lost
at an early period in the history of Irish might well be drawn
in such a situation, and, in this case, such a hypothesis would
be entirely correct. Although the occurrence of *p* in the phonemic inventory of prehistoric Irish is highly likely, the establishment of its occurrence in specific morphemes demands
other kinds of evidence.

In situations where the analyst is confronted with linguistic forms that are exceptional with respect to the prevailing structural patterns in a language (3), the method of internal reconstruction is often extraordinarily powerful. As an example of this type of internal analysis, let us consider a brilliant example provided by the Swiss linguist Ferdinand de Saussure in 1879 and much later confirmed by direct evidence.

THE INTERNAL RECONSTRUCTION OF INDO-EUROPEAN LARYNGEALS

Saussure investigated the structure of roots in reconstructed Proto-Indo-European. For the most part, roots were of the shape CVC—consonant – vowel – consonant (CVC)—or CVRC—consonant – vowel – resonant – consonant. The basic form of the vowel in both types was e, and there was the possibility that the resonant in type CVRC might occur in prevocalic position, as CeC, CeRC, or CReC (C includes all R). These forms (in part) represent the so-called *normal grade* of an IE root. Under specifiable morphological conditions, all of these root types can occur without the root vowel. This form is called the *zero grade* of the root. In such cases, a consonantal resonant will become vocalic if it happens to fall between two consonants. Some examples follow:

(3.4)

Normal/Zero (PIE)		Normal (Skt.) (1st sg. perfect indic. active)	Zero (Skt.) (1st sg. perfect indic. medio-passive)	(Past Partici
*bher/bhr ~ bhr̥	'carry'	ba·bhar·a	ba·bhr·e	bhr̥·ta
*ǵém/ǵm ~ ǵm̥	'go'	ja·gam·a	ja·gm·e	ga·ta (
*mei̯/mi ~ mi	'fix'	mi·may·a	mi·my·e	mi·ta
*ḱleu̯/ḱlu̯ ~ ḱlu	'hear'	śu·śrav·a	śu·śr(u)v·e	śru·ta
*deiḱ/diḱ	'point'	di·deś·a (*ei̯>e)	di·diś·e	diṣ·ṭa
*i̯euk^{u̯}/i̯uk^{u̯}	'join'	yu·yoj·a (*eu̯>o) (3rd sg. present indic. active)	yu·yuj·e (3rd sg. injunctive)	yuk·ta
*pet/pt	'fly'	pat·ati	pa·pt·at	

These alternations represent part of a more complex series of alternations in Indo-European termed *ablaut*. On the basis of data like these, we can say that there existed in Indo-European a morphophonemic alternation between *e* and ∅ with concomitant vocalization of a resonant in the zero grade alternant, whenever that resonant comes to occur in interconsonantal position as a result of the deletion of the root vowel.

A small number of widely attested and frequently used roots constitute an apparent exception to the general pattern just described. In such roots there is only one consonant, and in morphemes where that consonant is initial, the vowel of the root is *long* in normal grade contexts; moreover, the root vowel can be of three qualities—ē, ā, or ō. In zero grade contexts, that is to say, in grammatical situations where roots of the standard type delete the root vowel, a short vowel, reconstructed as *ə, occurs. This *ə is a hypothetical construct used to represent the prototype for the correspondence: *a* in most Indo-European languages; *i* in Indic and Iranian; *e, a,* or *o* in Ancient Greek. This root type is illustrated as follows:

(3.5)

Normal/Zero (PIE)		(1st sg. present indic. active)		/	(passive particle)	
		Sanskrit	Greek		Sanskrit	Greek
*dhē/dhə	'place'	da·dhā·mi	ti·thē·mi	/	hi·ta	the·to
*stā/stə	'stand'	ti·ṣṭhā·mi	hi·stā·mi	/	sthi·ta	sta·to
*dō/də	'give'	da·dāmi	di·dō·mi	/	di·ta	do·to

In 1879 Saussure suggested that it would be reasonable to assume that the class of roots characterized by a long vowel in alternation with *ə* were at one time structurally consistent with the more common type of root, and that phonetic changes had obscured this earlier identity. As we have seen, in standard roots ablaut resulted in the root vowel alternations schematized as follows:

(3.6)

Normal	Zero
e	Ø
ei	i
eu	u
er	r
el	l
em	m
en	n

If *ə* is inserted into the zero grade column above, we would predict a normal grade alternant, **eə*. Saussure noted that this must have been the original form of the alternation, i.e., *eə/ə*, and that postvocalic *ə* must have been lost through phonetic change with compensatory lengthening of the preceding vowel, i.e. **eə > ē*. In this way, a new alternation *ē ~ ə* is introduced into the language. Furthermore, Saussure postulated more than one *ə* in order to account for the various qualities of the long vowels which occur in the normal grade. He called these reconstructed segments *coéfficients sonantiques*.

It is interesting to note that Saussure's hypothesis drew little attention in the decades that followed its exposition. Forty-eight years later, in 1927, after the Hittite language had been discovered in Turkish Anatolia in 1906 and been deciphered by B. Hrozný in 1915, the Polish linguist Jerzy Kuryłowicz conclusively established the existence of Saussure's *coéfficients sonantiques*, now called *laryngeals*. He did so by pointing out that certain Hittite morphemes clearly cognate with morphemes in other IE languages show actual segments (written *h*, *ḫḫ*), otherwise unknown in Indo-European, in many positions where *coéfficients sonantiques* would be predicted by Saussure's hypothesis, as in Hitt. *laḫḫ-u* compared with Gk. *lā-os*. Thus a reconstruction based entirely on theoretical considerations and internal analysis was confirmed through subsequently discovered comparative evidence.

THE RELATIONSHIP BETWEEN THE COMPARATIVE METHOD AND INTERNAL RECONSTRUCTION

Internal reconstruction is a procedure for inferring only *part* of the history of a language, and so the results of internal methods of analysis are quite different from those of the comparative method. The comparative method attempts, ideally, to reconstruct a full synchronic system, or more realistically some subpart of that system such as the phonemic inventory or the set of inflectional endings for a prehistoric language assumed to have existed. Whereas stages in the histories of languages are recovered by means of the comparative method, specific historical events and individual features of ancestral grammars are recovered through internal reconstruction. To take an example, the comparison of cognate morphemes and cognate phonological systems permits the reconstruction of a parent phonological system and a lexicon of parent morphemes. Sound changes are coincidentally inferred on the basis of the relationship between the extant forms and the hypothetical forms from which they are assumed to be derived. On the other hand, the analysis of a particular phonological feature in a single language permits the direct recovery of the event—the sound change that accounts for that particular synchronic feature. Such an analysis, however, offers little or no detailed information about the larger system in which that event took place.

The term *prelanguage*, as distinct from protolanguage, is generally used to refer to a period in the history of a language associated with a certain feature reconstructible through internal reconstruction, or with a given linguistic change (or series of changes) reflected in a synchronic system, extant or reconstructed. Thus, in an explication of the recovery of intervocalic *s* in prehistoric Greek, the change $s > \emptyset / V$ ___ V may be relegated to the Pre-Greek period. Similarly, the merger of *a* and *o* as *a*, which differentiates the short vowel system of Proto-Germanic and that of Proto-Indo-European, must be considered a sound change that took place in Pre-Germanic, the reflex of which is realized in reconstructed

Proto-Germanic. In terms of the family tree model of linguistic differentiation, the nodes of the tree can be thought to represent protolanguages and extant languages, whereas the lines that connect those nodes refer to prelanguage periods. Of course, it must be remembered that a line of indefinite length can be drawn up from the node representing an ultimately reconstructed ancestor to a family, as internal reconstruction permits the recovery of changes which predate the existence of even these ancient prototypes. (Recall Saussure's reconstruction of the *coéfficients sonantiques*.) The term *common language* is also often seen in the historical linguistics literature. For example, the term Common Slavic refers to that stage in the historical development of the Slavic language that immediately preceded dialectal differentiation.

The relationship between internal reconstruction and the comparative method as practical procedures for linguistic reconstruction should be considered. Of course, when the linguist is concerned with the prehistory of a language with no known relatives, internal reconstruction is the only tool available. But it is more commonly the case that related languages do exist, and in such situations procedural decisions must be made. Is one method to be used to the exclusion of the other in a given investigation? If not, which procedure has priority with respect to order of application or to the accuracy of results? As might be expected, there are no easy answers to these questions, and linguists must use their own judgment in individual cases. If, for example, one of several sister languages shows an alternation unparalleled elsewhere in the family, internal reconstruction should be used to determine the more archaic form of the alternating morphemes. These forms can then be used for the establishment of correspondence sets in comparative analyses. If internal reconstruction did not take precedence in such a situation, historical comparison would be hindered by a clutter of forms resulting from late and language-specific developments, which give little or no insight into how to reconstruct a parent language. It should not, however, be construed that the moral to be drawn here is that internal reconstruction always precedes comparative analysis. On the contrary, there are many situations in which the opposite course is indicated. The history of the Slavic languages offers an example.

The morphophonemic systems of all the Slavic languages show the results of at least three, but probably four, separate but chronologically ordered palatalizations. For most, if not all, Slavic languages an insightful linguist should be able to reconstruct this series of sound changes on the basis of internal evidence alone. There exist sufficient data in the morphological system of Old Church Slavic, or in that of Russian, to permit the recovery of a prehistoric phonological system without palatal consonants. If the full potential of internal reconstruction were realized for each Slavic language, it is possible that palatal consonants could be eliminated from every one before a comparative analysis might be undertaken. Such a procedure would be very unfortunate. The palatalizations represent the most striking set of phonological innovations *shared* by all Slavic languages. It is unlikely that these several languages would share four conditioned sound changes in the same historical order (and, incidentally, showing the same relative chronology with respect to other shared developments) as the result of parallel innovation. It is far more reasonable to assume that these developments are Pre-Slavic, or that they are, at the latest, associated with the period of Slavic dialectal differentiation.

The methodological assumption, often presented in the linguistic literature, that internal reconstruction is always prerequisite for and independent of comparative method is clearly mistaken, as the Slavic data show. It is theoretically possible to reconstruct for any synchronic system a prelanguage devoid of morphophonemic alternation. If this were actually done, morphophonemic alternations (or phonological rules) would, by definition, be unreconstructible for any protolanguage. This is an unacceptable constraint to place on a natural language. Hence a procedural methodology that places such a constraint on protolanguages is also unacceptable, since it is assumed that protolanguages attempt to mirror actual linguistic systems.

RECOMMENDED READING

Anttila, R. (1968) "The Relation between Internal Reconstruction and the Comparative Method," *Ural-Altaische Jahrbücher* 40, 159–173.

Chafe, W. L. (1959) "Internal Reconstruction in Seneca," *Language* 35, 477–495.

de Saussure, F. (1887) Memoir *On the Primitive System of Vowels in the Indo-European Languages. Mémoire sur le système primitif des voyelles dans les langues indo-européennes,* authorized reprint of the 1879 edition, Vieweg, Paris.

Hoenigswald, H. M. (1944) "Internal Reconstruction," *Studies in Linguistics* 2, 78–87.

CHAPTER FOUR
MORPHOLOGICAL SYSTEMS AND
LINGUISTIC CHANGE

In the last chapter it was pointed out that internal reconstruction frequently involves the examination of morphophonemic alternations within a paradigm. The paradigm apparently has a psychological reality for language users that permits it to function as the domain for certain processes of linguistic change. One such process tends to eliminate the very paradigmatic alternations used as the primary data of internal reconstruction. Such a historical process, which reduces or completely eliminates allomorphy under specific paradigmatic conditions, is termed *leveling* or *paradigmatic leveling*. The term leveling is appropriate since alternations that are the result of phonetic change are eliminated or leveled out, and uniformity is restored to the paradigm. As a consequence of leveling, linguistic reconstruction through the method of internal reconstruction is often hindered or made impossible.

EFFECTS OF PARADIGMATIC LEVELING

As an example of paradigmatic leveling, consider the following innovation in the history of one Ancient Greek dialect. In earliest Greek (Pre-Greek) considerable allomorphy was present in the inflectional paradigm of so-called *i*-stem nouns. Historically at least three variants of this stem type were inherited from the parent language, Proto-Indo-European: *poli-, pole-* (< *$polei$-*), *polē-* (< *$polēi$-*) (i was lost in Greek intervocalically). Although the language of Homeric poetry does not necessarily reflect the situation in Pre-Greek in all its details, the following possible Homeric Greek paradigm exemplifies the alternation:

(4.1)

	Homeric Gk.	Doric Gk.
nom. sg.	poli-s	poli-s
acc.	poli-n	poli-n
gen.	pole-os	poli-os
dat.	polē-i	poli-i

voc.	poli	poli
nom/voc. pl.	pole-es/polē-es	poli-es
acc.	pole-ns	poli-ns
gen.	pole-ōn	poli-ōn
dat.	pole-si	poli-si

On the other hand, if we consider the corresponding paradigm for the Doric dialect of Ancient Greek, it becomes apparent that the alternation once present in the *i*-stem paradigm has been eliminated entirely. In Doric the stem alternant in *i*- has been generalized throughout.

As a consequence of leveling, it is often, though not necessarily, the case that a linguistic form that had been replaced historically due to phonetic change is restored. On the surface it might appear that a sound change is reversed. A consideration of the language as a whole, however, will make clear that the apparent reversal has occurred only under grammatically determined conditions, quite frequently within a paradigm. The history of the Russian imperative offers a straightforward example of such a phenomenon. In Old Church Slavic and Old Russian the second person singular imperative form ended in *-i*, which is derived from Pre-Slavic and PIE *-oi*. This *-i* < *-oi* was among the segments conditioning the so-called second regressive palatalization of Slavic, according to which $k > c$, and $g > (d)z$. Thus, the imperatives of the verbs *nesti* 'to carry', and *delati* 'to do' (infinitive ending *-ti*), were *nesi* and *delaj*, respectively. The imperatives of *pomogti* 'to help' and *vlekti* 'to drag' were *pomo(d)zi* and *vleci*, showing the reflexes of the palatalization.

In fourteenth-century Russian, the velar consonants began to be restored in the context of other forms in the verb paradigm that were not affected by the palatalization (like the infinitives *pomogat'* and *(pri)vlekat'*, the 1st sg. pres. forms *pomogaju* and *(pri)vlekaju*). In Modern Standard Russian, the imperatives *pomogi* and *(pri)vleki* are regular. It is worth emphasizing that the results of the second palatalization are not generally reversed in Russian. This apparent reversal is the consequence of paradigmatic regularization. It is not due to any form of phonetic change or phonetic reversion.

In the two examples of leveling just discussed, the paradigmatic context in which the innovation takes place is the morphological (or form) class (such as *i*-stem nouns). In a similar manner, standardization in the marking of some grammatical category may develop across morphological paradigm classes. In such cases the paradigmatic context in which leveling takes place is the grammatical category (such as accusative singulars of nouns). Greek again offers a good example. In Ancient Greek a final *-n* < **-m* occurs in all accusative singular forms, except in consonant stems (*tamian* 'treasure', *polin* 'city', *lukon* 'wolf'—but *patera* 'father', *Hellada* 'Greek'). This final *-a* in *patera* and *Hellada* is historically cognate with the *-n* of words like *tamian*; *patera* < *paterm. The original accusative singular ending *-m* is realized as a vowel when final after a consonant; it ultimately becomes *-a* by phonetic change. In Modern Greek the accusative singular ending *-n* has been generalized to all nouns; Modern Greek has *pateran* and *Hellaðan*. Allomorphy in the form of the accusative singular morpheme has been "leveled out."

CONTAMINATION

One special class of changes appears to be related to leveling in a certain sense, but its domain is neither the morphological nor grammatical paradigm. It often happens that the phonetic shape of a word or morpheme is changed in such a way that it becomes more like some other word or morpheme in a situation where both words and morphemes belong to a class defined by some close semantic relationship. We might consider this type of change a form of leveling within a semantic paradigm. The traditional term for such changes is *contamination*. English offers a good example. The Modern English word *father* /faðər/ cannot be derived in a regular manner from PIE and Pre-Germanic *patér*. PIE medial *t* became Proto-Germanic *þ* [θ] when accent preceded. Otherwise it became ð. In turn, ð became Old English (OE) *d*, so that the OE form was *fæder*, Middle English *fader*. Medial dental stops have undergone no further modification since the Middle English period, and the Modern English form should have intervocalic *d*. It is generally assumed that a substitution was made ($d \rightarrow \delta$), because *father* belongs to a semantic set that includes such words as *brother* < PIE $b^h r\acute{a}t\bar{e}r$, where intervocalic δ is derivable from PIE t in a regular manner.

Contamination is particularly common in words that generally occur in lists. For example, English *four* should not have initial f (compare it with Lat. *quattuor*, Skt. *catvaras*). The f is introduced under the influence of the number *five*, where initial f is the regular reflex of the first Germanic consonant shift (compare with Gk. *pente* or Skt. *pañca*). Similarly, the d in Russian (and Slavic in general) *dev'at'* 'nine' is unexpected (compare with Lat. *novem*, Skt. *navam*, Eng. *nine*). This d apparently reflects contamination from *des'at'* 'ten'. In Old Irish (OIr) contamination even affects the complex system of morphophonemics of that language.

In Pre-Celtic, the ancestor of Old Irish, under certain syntactic conditions, certain initial consonants underwent change when the preceding word ended with a nasal. For example, initial voiceless consonants became voiced when preceded by a word-final nasal. Final syllables are lost in Irish, and with them, of course, went final nasal consonants. But the effects on following words remained in the language. Hence, when a word like *secht* 'seven' (from **septm̥*) is followed by a word like *cenela* /kenela/ 'tribes', the sequence is realized as *secht genela*. The numbers *nói* 'nine' and *deich* 'ten' have the same effect, since they are historically derived from forms with a final nasal, **novem*, **deḱm̥*. Irish *ocht* 'eight' should not cause voicing of a following initial voiceless consonant, because historically it had no final nasal (**oktō*). However, voicing does occur after OIr. *ocht*, apparently a result of contamination from the words for seven, nine, and ten.

In all of the changes discussed thus far in this chapter, one or more allomorphs have been eliminated from the system in order to bring uniformity to the representation of a morpheme or class of morphemes. However, it is often the case that, while allomorphy is not reduced or eliminated, there occurs a change in the distribution of the alternants within some

paradigmatic context. Such innovations often result where the
conditions originally responsible for the introduction of some
morphophonemic alternation have become obscured by subsequent change. Consider the history of Sanskrit nouns with
stem-final velar stops.

In Pre-Indic the following sound change operated:

(4.2)

$$k, g > c \text{ [tš]}, j \text{ [dž]} / \underline{\hspace{2em}} \begin{Bmatrix} i \\ e \\ y \end{Bmatrix}.$$

Consequently in the inflection of the word *vāk* 'voice' < Pre-
Indic *u̯ōk*, an alternant *u̯ōc* is apparently introduced under the
conditions of the sound change. See columns A and B of the
following paradigm:

(4.3)

	A	B	C	D
nom. sg.	u̯ōk	u̯ōk	vāk	vāk
gen. sg.	u̯ōk-es	u̯ōc-es	vāc-as	vāc-as
inst. sg.	u̯ōk-ē	u̯ōc-ē	vāc-ā	vāc-ā
loc. sg.	u̯ōk-i	u̯ōc-i	vāc-i	vāc-i
nom. pl.	u̯ōk-es	u̯ōc-es	vāc-as	vāc-as
gen. pl.	u̯ōk-ōm	u̯ōk-ōm	vāk-ām	vāc-ām
inst. pl.	u̯ōg-bhis	u̯ōg-bhis	vāg-bhis	vāg-bhis
loc. pl.	u̯ōk-ṣi	u̯ōk-ṣi	vāk-ṣi	vāk-ṣi

A subsequent phonetic change produced the coalescence of *ĕ*
ŏ, *ă* as *ă*. As a result, the distribution of the alternant with a
palatal affricate is no longer predictable on phonetic grounds;
compare inst. sg. *vācā* and gen. pl. **vākām* (column C of
(4.3)). At this hypothetical stage in the history of Sanskrit,
speakers would apparently be forced to memorize the cases
in which one or the other alternant is to be used. However, in
Classical Sanskrit the allomorphs of this morpheme (and all
stems ending in a velar stop) have been redistributed, with a
resultant simplification in the statement of the distribution
(column D of (4.3)). In Classical Sanskrit the alternant ending

with a palatal occurs before all endings beginning with a vowel or resonant.

ANALOGY

A vast number and great variety of linguistic changes discussed in historical linguistics have been attributed to a linguistic process known as *analogy*. Although analogy has often been carelessly used as an historical explanation for various apparent anomalies in synchronic systems, many genuine cases of analogy are to be noted in the histories of languages.

The term analogy was first introduced by the Greeks (Gk. ἀναλογια, Lat. *proportio*) as a mathematical term to describe four-term propositions of the type a:b::c:d. Both the Greeks and the Romans also used the term in a transferred sense to account for complexes of similar relationships in languages. Consider Varro's definition of linguistic analogy in terms of a four-member proportion.

If there are two things of the same class which belong to some relation though in some respect unlike each other, and if alongside these two things two other things which have the same relation are placed, then because the two sets of words belong to the same *Lógos* each one is said separately to be an analogue and the comparison of the four constitutes an *Analogía*.

In genuine cases of historical analogy, on the basis of a preexisting structural pattern in a language, corresponding new patterns are introduced, by *analogic creation*, or old patterns are replaced, by *analogic extension*. Consequently the proportional model of the ancients traditionally has been used to characterize such analogic developments. Consider the two cases of analogic extension, one in the inflection of Old Church Slavic feminine *r*-stem nouns, shown in paradigms (4.4), the second in the inflection of certain Gothic consonant-stem (C-stem) nouns, shown in a subsequent example. (In (4.4) in cases where = appears in the center column, the equivalence in endings is the fortuitous result of sound change; where → appears, there has been an extension of the *i*-stem ending to C-stems.)

(4.4)

	i-stem (fem.)			C-stem (fem.)	
nom. sg.	kostĭ	'bone'	·	mati	'mother'
acc.	kostĭ		=	materĭ	
gen.	kosti			matere	
dat.	kosti		→	materi	
loc.	kosti		→	materi	
inst.	kostĭyǫ		→	materĭyǫ	
nom. pl.	kosti		→	materi	
acc.	kosti		=	materi	
gen.	kostii			materŭ	
dat.	kostĭmŭ		→	materĭmŭ	
loc.	kostĭxŭ		→	materĭxŭ	
inst.	kostĭmi		→	materĭmi	

Note that the feminine r-stem nouns are inflected in a manner difficult to distinguish from the manner in which the feminine i-stem nouns are inflected. Historically such was not the case, and the prominence of -i- and -ĭ- in the r-stem paradigm suggests that i-stem endings have been extended to consonant stem nouns. Two important questions need to be answered at this point. Why should the original endings of consonant-stems have been replaced at all, and once that is explained, why should the i-stem endings have been extended over the endings of any other morphological class, such as o-stems, jo-stems, or ā-stems?

The answer to the first question is somewhat complicated, but suffice it to say that the introduction of a new syllable structure constraint in Slavic, the so-called law of open syllables, demanded the elimination of all internal consonant clusters, including those that would result from the juxtaposition of a noun stem ending in a consonant and a desinence beginning with a consonant. Several such situations would arise in the inflection of Slavic consonant stems, like feminines in r-. It is the answer to the second question—why the i-stems should have been extended—that is more germane to the present discussion.

Historical analogy being the extension of some preexisting pattern to a new situation, if this extension of *i*-stem endings is to be explained in terms of analogy, it is necessary to establish such a pattern. In this case, such a pattern is present. The Proto-Indo-European ending for accusative singular was *-*m*. In Slavic the word-final sequence -*im* becomes -*ĭ* by regular phonetic change. Hence, the *i*-stem acc. sg. *kostĭ* is regular, as shown in (4.4). Final -*m* after a consonant is syllabic in the parent language, that is *-*m̥*, and in Slavic *m̥ becomes *ĭ* via *-*ĭm*. Hence, the accusative singular *materĭ* is also regular. In this way fortuitous identity is established for fem. *i*-stem and *r*-stem nouns in the accusative singular. It is this pattern of identity that is generalized; the development of the locative is an example:

(4.5)
kostĭ   :   materĭ   :   :   kostĭxŭ   :   X
                                        X → materĭxŭ

The analogic extension in Gothic is far more restricted in its scope, but we think especially instructive as a result. In the Gothic nominal system, certain C-stems, including *r*-stems, show a nominative plural ending that is clearly not the expected reflex. For example, the nominative plural of *brôþar* 'brother' is *brôþrjus*. The ending -*jus* is totally unexpected in an *r*-stem noun, but quite obviously it corresponds to the historically expected termination for *u*-stem nouns, such as *sunus* 'son', which has a nominative plural, *sunjus*. One might ask the following questions: Why is the *u*-stem ending generalized, rather than the nominative plural of any other nominal class? Why has the *u*-stem formative -*jus* been extended only to the *r*-stems and to no other classes? Can the encroachment of the *u*-stem ending be an arbitrary development?

The answers to these questions are to be found in the explication of the analogic context that apparently motivated the innovation in *r*-stem inflection. The result of the Gothic innovation is formal identity in the nominative plural of masculine *u*- and *r*-stems. What is crucial is that the pattern for

such identity had already been established in the accusative plural forms of these two noun classes. The inherited accusative plural ending is *-ns*, and the historical derivation of the accusative plural of *u*-stems is straightforward: *sunu + ns →
sununs*. In Germanic, however, a vocalic resonant develops into the sequence *u* plus the consonantal alternant of the resonant. Consequently, Gothic *brôþruns < *bhrātr + ns* is the expected reflex of a C-stem accusative plural, since the *n* of *-ns* is syllabic between consonants and develops into *-un*. Once the fortuitous identity of accusative plural forms like *sununs* and *brôþruns* is established, what might have appeared to be an arbitrary morphological extension becomes a highly constrained and well-motivated development.

(4.6)
sununs : sunjus : : brôþruns : X
                                  X → brôþrjus

It has already been noted that analogic developments include not only the extension of old formatives to new contexts but also the introduction of entirely novel forms. In cases where the latter is true, we may speak of analogic creation.

ANALOGIC CREATION

One example of analogic creation comes from Armenian, which inherits an *aorist indicative* construction in both the *active* and *middle* voices, as shown by first singular aorist indicative active *beri* 'I have carried' and the first singular aorist indicative middle *beray* 'I have carried'. The language also inherits a series of forms synchronically constituting the category *aorist subjunctive active,* like the first singular aorist subjunctive active *beric'*. Historically, this category probably reflects an optative mood form enlarged with the suffix *-ske/
o*. These old optatives have apparently undergone a semantic shift causing them to become the subjunctive correspondents to indicative actives of the type *beri*. No corresponding *aorist subjunctive middle* is inherited from the parent language; thus a gap is left in the system. The gap is eliminated, however,

through the operation of analogical creation, where

(4.7)
beri : beray : : beric' : X
                              X → berayc'

The introduction of a formation like *berayc'* (and the full
paradigm associated with it) can only be explained in the
context of preexisting patterns.

A similar analogic creation occurs in Hittite, an ancient
language of the Indo-European family. In Hittite there exist
two lexical categories of verbs. These two classes are distinguished most notably by the form of the first person singular
ending in the present tense. For one group of verbs that ending
is -*mi*; for the other, it is *ḫi* (*ḫ* represents some postvelar
continuant). The endings -*mi* and -*ḫi* correspond to the first
person singular (1st. sg.) endings in presential aspect and perfective aspect in other IE languages, respectively. In Hittite
1st. sg. ending for -*mi* type verbs is -*un*. The ending -*un* corresponds to -*m*, a well-known 1st sg. ending in other IE languages. The 1st sg. ending for the preterite of -*hi* type verbs
is -*hun*. The ending *hun* has no correspondent in related languages, and is not derived from PIE. It apparently represents
a Hittite creation based on the analogic pattern

(4.8)
mi : ḫi : : un : X
                    X → ḫun

MORPHOLOGICAL REINTERPRETATION
New morphemes may also be introduced into a linguistic system through various processes of *morphological reinterpretation*. In one type of reinterpretation historical events conspire to necessitate an alteration in the grammatical function
of a morpheme. This process is called *regrammatization*.
Consider, for example, the origin of the German plural
marker, -*er*.

In Indo-European there is a class of neuter nouns formed
with the derivational suffix **-e/os-*. The nominative/accusative
singular (nom./acc. sg.) of such neuter nouns shows no inflec-

tional ending. In the nominative/accusative plural, the desinence is historically *-*ā*; for example, sg. *root-*es* becomes pl. *root-*es*-*ā*. In Germanic most word-final vowels and some word-final sequences of short vowel plus a consonant were lost. Consequently, in the nom/acc. of Old High German neuter *s*-stems, the derivational suffix -*es*, being word-final, has been lost completely, although this suffix remains in the plural, where the desinence has been lost. Hence, we find Old High German (OHG) sg. *lamb* 'lamb', pl. *lembir* and Middle High German (MHG) *lamp, lember.* (The vowel change is due to Germanic umlaut.)

Faced with this new situation the speakers of Old High German apparently had little choice but to reinterpret the suffix -*ir* (corresponding to Middle High German -*er*) as the plural marker. Subsequently, this innovative pattern is generalized analogically to other neuter nouns, particularly the reflexes of PIE neuter *o*-stems like *wort*, where the loss of final syllables left the singular and plural indistinguishable. Hence OHG/MHG sg. *wort*, pl. *wort* → Modern Standard German *Wort, Wörter*.

The most widely discussed form of morphological reanalysis is the generally sporadic and analogic process termed *back formation*. Innovative formations of the type *denotate* for *denote* and *connotate* for *connote* are "back formed" from *denotation* and *connotation* on the basis of the pattern apparent in *levitate/levitation, decapitate/decapitation*, and perhaps even similar but not entirely corresponding pairs of the type *eliminate/elimination*.

Two widely cited cases of back formation in the history of English result because in Middle English, -*s* became the general plural marker. When certain foreign words were borrowed into English with stem-final -*s*, the -*s* was analogically interpreted as a plural marker and innovative singular morphemes were created. For example, Latin *pisum*, which was borrowed into English, first became *pes*, later yielding English *pease*; the current singular *pea* is the result of back formation. In a similar manner, Old French *cherise* has given Modern English *cherry*.

Folk etymology is a type of innovation closely related to back formation. Folk etymology is characterized by the reinterpretation of words whose surface morphology has become synchronically opaque by means of words or morphemes that are more familiar. The treatment of the English word *hamburger* illustrates the notion of folk etymology. In German, adjectives may be derived from place names with the suffix *-er*. Many place names are compounds with *-burg* as the second element. Thus *Hamburger* is an adjective derived from the name of the city *Hamburg*; *Berliner* and *Wiener* are adjectives derived from *Berlin* and *Wien*, respectively; and *Frankfurter* is derived from *Frankfurt*. Such an adjective would normally occur with a noun, as in *Wiener Würstchen* 'Vienna sausages'. In English, however, the meaningless *ham* of *Hamburg* must have been reinterpreted as 'ham', or at least as some kind of meat (although hamburgers are rarely, if ever, made of ham) in the borrowed word *hamburger*. The reanalysis has given rise to numerous other *burgers*, such as *cheeseburger* and *fishburger,* all of which may be bought at places with names like *Burger King*. Similarly *asparagus* has become *sparrowgrass* in some English dialects, and *Infanta of Castile* has given *Elephant and Castle,* the name of a famous pub in Old London.

Morphemic reanalysis of the types seen in back formations often has a far more regular and profound effect on the morphological and morphosyntactic system of a language than happens to be the case in the preceding examples. A completely novel and subsequently productive grammatical morpheme may be introduced simply as a result of misperception—or perhaps better, an altered perception—of the placement of morphemic boundaries. In situations of this type, it is important to note that the generalization—indeed, the very existence of the innovative structural entity—appears to represent an arbitrary development unless some perceptual motivation for the original reanalysis can be established. Commonly, such motivation is analogical. The development of the Latin infinitive is a case in point.

It is widely assumed that the Latin active infinitive in *-re*

finds its origin as an *s*-stem noun in the locative case (*-re* <
-si). The final vowel of *-re* reflects the regular phonetic development, *i* > *e* / ___ #, and rhotacism occurs in Latin,
hence *-r-* in *-re* < PIE *-s-*. Yet, first-, second-, and fourth-
conjugation Latin infinitives, like *amāre* 'to love', *monēre* 'to
advise', and *audīre* 'to hear', as well as radical (root) infinitives like *esse* 'to be', offer some difficulty inasmuch as PIE
shows no nouns with suffixation of the types *-ās-*, *-ēs-*, *-īs-*, or
-s-. Such suffixes ending in *-s* would be necessary in order to
interpret most Latin infinitives as straightforward reflexes of
s-stem nouns, since the only suffix ending in *-s* in PIE is of
the form *-es*.

Latin infinitives of the third conjugation, however, are less
awkward. If we project backward to the Pre-Latin form of a
third-conjugation infinitive such as *dūcere*, we note for Pre-
Latin **doukesi* formal identity with the locative case of a
genuine Indo-European *s*-stem noun. Hence, we have apparently established an historical explanation of some Latin infinitives, but the question remains as to how the *s* of the original
derivational suffix comes to be disassociated from the preceding vowel *e*, giving a productive suffix **-si* > *-re*, as in *amāre*.

A motivation for this apparent morphological reanalysis can
be established if we recognize the striking similarity between
that portion of the old *s*-stem noun preceding the innovative
infinitive suffix and the verbal stem of the thematic (*-e* suffixed) third conjugation. The process of reinterpretation that
accounts for the new Latin infinitives probably begins with
the analogic reanalysis of *s*-stem nouns like Pre-Latin **douk-
+es+i,* as **douk-e+si* on the basis of related thematic verbal
forms of the type **douk-e+s* (2nd. sg. pres.) > *dūcis* (2nd. sg.
pres.); **douk-e+t* > *dūcit*. This newly established verbal suffix, **-si* (> *-re*), becomes productive and is extended to all
verbal stems, giving *amāre* < **amā+si, monēre* < **monē+si,*
audīre < **audī+si,* and even *esse* from **es*, plus this newly
autonomous grammatical morpheme **-si*.

It is particularly important to emphasize the analogic basis
of the morphemic reanalysis. Without the establishment of
some context in which the first part of certain old verbal nouns

(such as *dūce-* < **douke-*) might come to be reinterpreted as a verbal stem, the generalization of **-si* would seem an arbitrary development. The analogic context offers both a motivation for the reinterpretation because it explains the very existence of **-si* (> *-re*) as a structurally autonomous entity of Latin grammar, and an explanation of the occurrence of *-si* in verbs like *amāre* as a secondary development.

It should be apparent at this point that we have restricted the widely used term analogy to instances of change that can be characterized in terms of a four-term proposition—a proportional model. In the literature of historical linguistics other types of change are often termed analogic. The term *analogic leveling*, for example, is widely used. However, it is important to differentiate between changes for which the model is furnished by other forms of the same word, and those for which corresponding forms of other words serve as a model.

In the Doric Greek leveling already discussed, one allomorph of a morpheme type has been generalized to all contexts. In order to characterize this development as an instance of genuine analogic change, it would be necessary to assume that the leveling was dependent on the preexistence in the Doric nominal inflectional system of a paradigm type in which there is no allomorphy in the shape of the stem. It is unlikely that such a model paradigm existed at the time of the Doric *i*-stem innovation. In any case, although such a model paradigm may sometimes exist in situations where leveling occurs, it seems especially demanding to require such a context. The characterization of leveling as a straightforward case of structural simplification seems appropriate. In most instances of leveling, one allomorphic variant is generalized so that complicated (and often synchronically unmotivated) alternations might be eliminated from the grammar. In analogy, some established structural pattern is generalized to novel contexts.

That analogy (or false analogy) is an inappropriate term to characterize all types of linguistic change that find their motivation in morphological association was first noted by Karl Brugmann in 1876. He suggested *Form-association* 'form-association' for the several types of change we have been discussing. Hermann Paul in his outstanding 1920 book, *Prinzipien der Sprachgeschichte,* made a clear distinction between leveling and analogy. The former he called *stoffliche Analogiebildung* 'material analogy', and the latter *formale Analogiebildung* 'formal analogy'. The distinction is certainly useful in terms of the typological classification of linguistic change, but, more important, it is significant with respect to historical linguistic explanation, as it makes reference to the ways formal categories are perceived by speakers.

ANALOGIC RESTORATION

As a result of certain of the developments discussed in this chapter, older forms having undergone phonetic change have been secondarily restored. *Analogic restoration* has been used to describe such developments. Indeed, there are many well-documented cases of genuine restoration. As an example, recall the case of the Russian imperative mentioned earlier—the restoration of velar consonants because of paradigmatic regularization. There is some controversy as to whether all such cases are to be explained as restorations. In other words, is it necessary to take the Neogrammarian tenet concerning sound change absolutely literally at all times, or might not analogic pressure sometimes serve as a constraint on the progress of regular sound change?

If we are working with written records there can be no doubt that analogic pressure has had effect, if the ''unrestored'' forms actually occur in texts. But there are countless cases where such data are simply not available. The development of certain Ancient Greek aorists is a good example. In intervocalic position PIE *s* is lost in Ancient Greek. Intervocalic -*s*- is the morpheme of aorist aspect in many IE languages, and it is added to verb-roots to give aorist stems. This aorist -*s*- should, by regular phonetic change, be lost in Greek in roots ending in vowels where the inflectional ending begins with a vowel. However, roots such as *lu*, from *luō* 'I loosen', offer aorists of the shape *elūsa* (1st sg.). It is widely assumed that this -*s*- has been analogically restored on the basis of aorists with consonant final roots, such as *edeik-s-a*. Yet, since there is no record of intermediate aorists without the intervocalic -*s*-, it might well be argued that the *s* of the *elūsa*, has been analogically retained, rather than analogically restored.

THE CONDITIONS FOR ANALOGIC CHANGE

There have been a number of attempts to determine principles for establishing conditions under which changes of the type discussed in this chapter might be precipitated. The most well known, and perhaps the best, such attempt was made by Jerzy Kuryłowicz in a 1940s article entitled "La nature des procés dits analogiques." The following are the four principles he proposed in that article.

1. A twofold morphological marker tends to replace one that is single. As an example, consider the -*e* plural of German nouns, which is also associated with umlaut in some nouns. Both the -*e* suffix and umlaut mark the plural in some nouns. This constitutes a twofold morphological marker. Umlaut is extended to other -*e* plurals where it did not originally occur. Thus on the analogy of *Gast/Gäste*, umlaut is extended to *Baum/Bäume* (originally *Baume*).

2. Analogy proceeds from base forms (*formes de fondation*) to derived forms (*formes fondées*). Consider the so-called fleeting vowels in Russian, which appear in the nominative, but are syncopated in certain oblique cases. The vowels are reintroduced into the oblique case forms by paradigmatic leveling. A regular alternation would be nom. sg. masc. *son* 'dream': gen. sg. masc. *sna* 'of the dream'. In a word like *zov* 'call', the genitive *zva* persisted until 1847, after which the innovative form *zova* began to spread.

3. Any construction consisting of a constant plus a variable is used as a pattern for an isolated entity in the same function. Thus in English, an adverb is normally formed from an adjective with the addition of the suffix -*ly*. There are isolated, monomorphemic adverbs as well; these tend to be replaced by pleonastic formations with -*ly*. The pattern is established by

correspondences like *wrong* : *wrongly* : : *slow* : X; X → *slowly*. From a historical point of view, *slow* might be expected to have the same history as *fast,* which still functions both as an adjective and an adverb. As another example recall the change from MHG sg. *wort* : pl. *wort* to MSG *Wort* : *Wörter.*

4. A new analogical form takes over the primary function of a contrast, while the replaced form is used for secondary functions. In English, for example, consider pairs like *brothers–brethren,* where the regularized form is the normal, semantically unmarked plural, while *brethren,* the replaced form, assumes a peripheral, specialized function. Similarly, the comparative *older* is the general form, while the replaced *elder* has a special and restricted meaning in Modern English.

CHANGES IN GRAMMATICAL CATEGORIES

Finally, we might briefly discuss two types of innovation altering the morphological system of a language by changing the number of grammatical categories that are morphologically marked in a given language. The two are *syncretism* and *morphologization.* Syncretism is the term used to describe developments whereby grammatical distinctions are eliminated. For example, it sometimes happens that phonetic change results in the ''accidental,'' but complete, loss of a grammatical distinction. More commonly, however, it is the case that a grammatical distinction is lost in one (or a few) morphological classes as a result of phonetic change, and subsequently, the pattern of identity is extended analogically. Such a development occurs in the history of Latvian nominal inflection.

In Proto-Baltic, nouns are formally distinguished in the accusative and instrumental cases of the singular. (Lithuanian, for example, retains this distinction.) For so-called *jo*-stem and *o*-stem nouns there existed in Baltic an accusative singular ending *-an*, and an instrumental singular ending *-u*. In Latvian, sequences of a vowel plus tautosyllabic *n* changed in such a way that this *n* became either *i* or *u*, corresponding in backness with the vowel that preceded it. This sequence was then metathesized, with a subsequent loss of the final vowel.

The accusative singular ending -*an*, for example, will undergo the following changes: **-an > au > ua > u*. Consequently, *(j)o*-stem nouns in Latvian come to be formally identical in the accusative and instrumental singular (a partial syncretism); *es redzu tẽvu* 'I see father': *es eju ar tẽvu* 'I go with father'.

Under the analogic influence of this identity in (j)o-stem nouns, the instrumental and accusative singular of all nouns ultimately fall together. In *ijo*-stems, for example, Old Latvian shows accusative singular -*i* (< **-ii* < **in*), and instrumental singular -*u*. But the accusative, -*i*, soon replaces the instrumental -*u*, giving identical forms in the two cases. The analogy apparently operated as follows:

(4.9)

acc. tẽvu 'father'   : inst. tẽvu : :
    brāli 'brother' :   X
                 X → brāli

Just as grammatical distinctions may be eliminated, they may also be introduced. Sometimes such an innovation is the result of analogic creation, as was the Armenian aorist subjunctive middle mentioned earlier. New grammatical categories may also result from the semantic differentiation of allomorphs. A development of this type may be termed *morphologization*. Some scholars believe that the distinction between dative and locative cases in many Indo-European languages is a result of morphologization.

As a consequence of the phenomenon of ablaut, many Indo-European morphemes have multiple shapes, as does Ancient Greek: *leip/loip/lip* 'leave'. The traditional reconstruction for the Indo-European dative singular ending is **-oi*, and for the locative singular it is **-i* (in Sanskrit -*e* < **-oi* : -*i* < **-i*). It might be suggested that **-oi* and **-i* had, at one time, the same kind of widely attested allomorphic relationship noted in Gk. *loip/lip*. Evidence in support of this suggestion would include such facts as the Greek use of -*i* < **-i* as a dative, rather than locative, case ending, and Old Persian -*oi* < **-oi* as a locative case marker. If this hypothesis is correct, a single PIE dative or locative ending with two morphophonemic alternants has, in at least some Indo-European languages, given two distinct category markers. An old, conditioned alternation has been morphologized.

RECOMMENDED READING

Andersen, H. (1976) "Towards a Typology of Change: Analogy," in *Proceedings of the Second International Conference on Historical Linguistics,* W. Christie, ed., *Current Progress in Historical Linguistics,* North Holland, Amsterdam.

Anttila, R. (1974) *Analogy,* Department of General Linguistics, University of Helsinki.

Benveniste, E. (1968) "Mutations of Linguistic Categories," in *Directions for Historical Linguistics,* W. P. Lehmann and Y. Malkiel, eds., University of Texas Press, Austin, Texas.

Bloomfield, L. (1933) *Language,* Holt, Rinehart and Winston, New York, chapter 23.

Jeffers, R. J. (1975) "On the Notion 'Explanation' in Historical Linguistics," in *Proceedings of the 1st International Conference on Historical Linguistics,* C. Anderson and C. Jones, eds., *Historical Linguistics,* North Holland, Amsterdam.

Jeffers, R. J. (1977) "Morphological Reanalysis and Analogy: Two Case Histories from Latin and Greek," *Lingua* 41, 13-41.

Kuryłowicz, J. (1945-59) "La nature des procés dits 'analogiques'." *Acta Linguistica* 5, 15-37.

Sapir, E. (1921) *Language,* Harcourt, Brace and World, New York, chapter 7.

Watkins, C. (1970) "A Further Remark on Lachmann's Law." *Harvard Studies in Classical Philology* 74, 55-66.

CHAPTER FIVE
PHONOLOGICAL CHANGE

Sound change may be considered in terms of simple phonetic change—as alterations in the manner whereby given segments or classes of segments are articulated from one point in the history of a language to another. We know, however, that the phonetic segments used by speakers of a language in the oral production of their language are organized into a highly structured system. The design of this *phonological system* is determined by the way in which various phonetic features function to establish distinctive oppositions and by a set of "rules" relating phonetically distinct but morphologically unique forms. In this chapter we will consider various types of developments that result in phonological change. The discussion will be organized in the context of the descriptive systems that some linguists have used to characterize phonological changes. The descriptive typologies of phonological change to which we will refer are those associated with American structuralism, Prague School structuralism, and generative grammar. The various theoretical biases associated with these three approaches to phonology serve to highlight important aspects of phonological change. At the same time, these biases often result in accounts of phonological change that, in each case, are not entirely adequate. An attempt is made here to integrate the valuable contributions that have come from these three sources.

Phonetic change, obviously, plays a primary role in phonological restructuring, but changes in other aspects of the grammar also have significant effects on the structural system. *Phonological restructuring* will be used here in the broadest sense to refer to any type of structural reorganization in the sound system of a language.

THE STRUCTURALISTS' APPROACH TO PHONOLOGY

As students of American structural linguistics turned their attention to linguistic change in general and sound change in particular, their interest centered around the ways in which a language's inventory of phonemes might come to be reorganized. How and when are new oppositions introduced or old ones lost? How and when does a realignment in the system of phonological contrasts take place? That is, under what circumstances do the phonological (or phonemic) representations of given morphemes change without concomitant change in the phonemic stock? Largely on the basis of the work of Henry Hoenigswald (1946, 1960), a system of classification for phonological change was developed. The terminology associated with this system is still widely used by historical linguists.

The basic premise of the structuralist system for classifying phonological change is that all forms of phonological restructuring begin with phonetic split or merger. As explained in chapter 3, merger may be partial (conditioned) or complete (unconditioned).

A complete merger results when two (or more) sounds fall together in all environments where they formerly contrasted. This may reflect a phonetic alteration of either or both of the phonemes involved. An unconditioned merger always results in a change in the phonological system, and that change is assumed to be irreversible. Where there was once two (or more) phonemes, after merger there is one, and its subsequent history will in no way reflect its multiple origins. The complete loss of a phonetic difference between two (or more) phonologically distinct segments has also been termed *absolute neutralization*.

The merger of Proto-Indo-European *o* and *a* as *a* in Germanic is unconditioned. Hence Gmc. *a* develops without regard to its dual history, as we would expect. It is interesting, however, that because of subsequent developments most Gmc. languages have a short vowel system that is typologically identical with that assumed for late PIE, namely, *i, e, a, o, u*. This is coincidental. Late in the Gmc. period, a sound change of the form u > o / _____ C(C) *a, ō* reintroduced *o*, as in OHG wolf < *wulfa-. In time this new *o* became phonemically distinct. Although a comparison of the phonemic inventories of PIE, Proto-Gmc. and Old High German suggests that a restructured system has reverted to its earlier makeup, an analysis of historical events demonstrates that such a *phonological reversion* is only apparent. Phonological reversion refers to the hypothetical situation whereby the results of phonological restructuring are undone, as, for example, if a contrast were reintroduced after a complete merger in all and only those lexical contexts where the contrast existed before the merger. Most historical linguists do not consider genuine phonological reversion to be a possible historical event.

The complete loss of a phoneme may be viewed as a case of unconditioned merger, or merger with zero. As is the case with other types of mergers, a possible phonological distinction in the lexicon is lost as a consequence of merger with zero. For example, Old Latin *h* was lost in Late Latin, with the result that a word like *hortus* 'garden' became homophonous with *ortus* 'origin'.

SPLIT

Conditioned merger necessarily coincides with phonetic split. If some tokens (allophones) of a phoneme /x/ merge with /y/, a conditioned split in /x/ has occurred. This phenomenon is termed *primary split*. Latin rhotacism is a well-known example. Pre-Latin *s* and *r* remain distinct in Classical Latin with the exception that the *s* coalesces with *r* (probably via *z*) in intervocalic position:

(5.1)
a. s. . . . . s (except as in b)
b. s - - :·r / V ____ V
c. r ÷ - - r

The dotted and broken lines represent the concomitant split in *s* and merger of *r* and *s*, respectively. The phonological consequence of primary split is a realignment in the system of phonological contrasts. The phonological representation of the Old Latin (OLat.) personal name *Valesius*, for example, includes a medial /s/, whereas its (Cl)Lat. reflex *Valerius* shows medial /r/. As a result of primary split the phonological representation of certain morphemes changes without any alteration in the inventory of phonemes.

Primary splits may arise in a variety of ways. Among these is an interesting type whereby unchanged segments are phonologically reinterpreted. The phenomenon has been called *primary split from reassignment*. In Germanic, for example, the IE voiceless stops become spirants in most environments as part of the historical change known as the First Germanic Consonant Shift (*p, t, k* > *f/v, θ/ð, x/γ*). However, after tautosyllabic *s*, these voiceless stops do not become spirants; compare English *stand*, Lat. *sto*, and Gk. *histāmi*. It will be recalled that the reconstructed IE voiced stops *b, d, g* are devoiced in Germanic, consequently reintroducing the phones *p, t, k* in most environments. The stops *p, t, k* of the inherited sequences *sp, st, sk* apparently come to be considered tokens of the new /p, t, k/ from */b, d, g/, rather than of the old */p, t, k/, which they historically reflect.

It is often the case that a phonetic split results in a change in the phonemic inventory only after a later change has taken place (resulting in a phonemic split). For example, the segment(s) that served to condition the original split themselves may undergo a change. This type of *secondary split* is very common, and we consider a few examples here.

It will be recalled that in the course of the prehistory of Sanskrit velar stops become palatal affricates in the environment of front vowels. Thus, Skt. *k* splits into *k* and *c* [tš]. But we have also noted that the front vowel *e* subsequently merges with *a* and *o* as *a*, with the result that tokens of the phone *c* come to occur in nonpalatal environments. In Sanskrit, the word *ca* 'and' from **ke* (< **kᵘe*), is distinguished from the root *ka* 'who, which' from **ko* (< **kᵘo*), by the quality of the initial consonant. A change elsewhere in the system has given phonemic status to a segment introduced into the system as a phonetically predictable alternant. This type of change may introduce complications into the system of paradigmatic alternations that can be seen in the many morphophonemic alternations considered in chapter 4.

A similar case of secondary split affects the alternants introduced by umlaut in Germanic. Old High German *a, o, u* are fronted to *ä, ö, ü* where *i* occurs in the following syllable, but all OHG short vowels merge as *ə* (spelled *e*) in unstressed final syllables. MHG *schone* 'already' from OHG *scōno* and MHG *schǽne* 'beautiful' from OHG *scōni* are distinguished by the difference in quality between *o* and *œ* (*ö*), which had earlier been a predictable alternant. In both the Sanskrit and Germanic examples synchronic alternations result in conditioned sound changes as a consequence of secondary split.

Secondary split may also occur when some development subsequent to a change introducing a phonetic alternation results in an expansion of the types of phonetic contexts in which one of the alternants may occur. In situations of this type, it is common that the secondary development is *not* a sound change. Paradigmatic leveling is often the source for this type of phonological change. If, in a language, a given phoneme *x* develops two phonetic alternants, *x'* / ___ Q and *y* elsewhere, it is likely that paradigms with the conditioned alternation *x'* ~ *y* will occur. It is then possible—at some later time in the history of the language, when the sound change that produced the alternations is no longer productive—that one of the alternants will spread to formerly precluded phonetic contexts as a result of some form of morphological or syntactic simplification. This is the phenomenon termed leveling. In virtually every instance leveling results in a restructured phonological system.

An expansion of the contexts in which a given segment occurs may also arise when tokens of that segment are introduced from some secondary source. Phonemic split often occurs in such cases. In Old English a series of phonetically predictable alternations occurred as a consequence of a phonetic split that voiced fricatives in intervocalic position. The alternants were *f/v*, *þ/ð*, *s/z*. Subsequently, medial geminate fricatives were simplified (*ff*, *þþ*, *ss* > *f*, *þ*, *s* / V ___ V). With the reintroduction of voiceless fricatives in intervocalic position, *f* and *v* and other pairs come to contrast, and a new phonological distinction is introduced.

THE PRAGUE SCHOOL OF PHONOLOGY

A similar categorization of phonological change, which was developed by Roman Jakobson (1931), is associated with the

Prague school of structural phonology. In this system, the two principal categories of phonological change are *dephonologization* and *phonologization,* which correspond roughly to merger and split, respectively. These two types of phonological change differ from merger and split in that they are not restricted to the system of phonological oppositions. The Prague School's phonology distinguishes between *phonological contrast,* the system of distinctive phonological oppositions, and *phonological correlation,* the system of relationships that hold between features characterizing classes of sounds. Hence, dephonologization may refer to the loss of a contrast and/or the loss of a correlation. For the most part, phonologization corresponds to secondary splits in the American structuralist system.

DEPHONOLOGIZATION

Although a dephonologization in the system of phonological oppositions generally results in the loss of both a phonological distinction and its corresponding phonetic contrast, that is not always the case. In certain Russian dialects unstressed /a/ and unstressed /e/, formerly separate phonemes, change into conditioned allophones of one phoneme: [e] appears after palatalized consonants, [a] after nonpalatalized consonants. Examples are *p'aták* 'five-kopeck coin' > *p'eták* and *žen'íx* 'bridegroom' > *žan'íx.* As a result of two sound changes, *a* > *e*/C' _____ and *e* > *a*/C _____, sounds that were formerly independent phonemes have become conditioned allophones of one phoneme, without loss of phonetic contrast.

More commonly, no phonetic distinction remains after dephonologization. In many branches of Indo-European (Baltic, Slavic, Iranian, Celtic), for example, the series of consonants termed aspirates **bh, *dh, *gh* fall together with the traditional voiced stops **b, *d, *g.* Hence, not only are there oppositions lost, but there is also a loss from the system of the phonological correlation (that is, the distinctive feature) by which *bh* and *b,* for example, were differentiated. It is important to recall, however, that all mergers do not result in losses of a correlation, even when the loss of a given phonetic distinction accompanies the loss of a contrast. In Ukrainian and Byelo-

russian r' and r coalesce; but the correlation of palatalized and
nonpalatalized has by no means disappeared, as there are
many other pairs of consonants where the palatalization opposition has not been lost.

PHONOLOGIZATION

The examples of secondary split given earlier all result in
phonologization. Latvian offers an example similar to the one
from Sanskrit that resulted in the introduction of the opposition k, g / c [tš], j [dž]. In Latvian, k, $g > c$, j / _____ front
vowels. In a subsequent development $ai > i$, resulting in a
situation whereby $ci < {}^*ki$ comes to be in phonetic opposition
with $ki < {}^*kai$. The allophones c and j are phonologized. Note
that the Latvian and the Sanskrit changes result not only in
the introduction of new phonemic oppositions, but also of a
new phonological correlation, of palatal and nonpalatal consonants. The feature [palatal] has been introduced into the
Latvian and Sanskrit phonological systems as a distinctive
feature.

As a result of another Latvian development we see the
introduction of a new opposition without any corresponding
change in the system of correlations. In Latvian the sequence
$l + j$ [į] becomes l' introducing a new phonemic opposition, l/
l'. Compare *bralis* 'brother' (nom. sg.), *bral'i* (nom. pl.) and
cirvis 'axe' (nom. sg.), *cirvji* (nom. pl.). Since there already
exists a phonemic distinction between palatalized and nonpalatalized consonants elsewhere in the system, this development has no effect on the system of correlations (distinctive
features).

REPHONOLOGIZATION

A third type of phonological change, *rephonologization*, is
also defined in the Prague School system. Rephonologization
occurs when a change creates a reorganization in the old
system of correlations without any decrease or increase in the
number of distinctive oppositions. The unconditioned change
from PIE ${}^*\acute{g} >$ Slavic z is an example. Slavic inherits s from
PIE. The correlation of the feature *voiced* versus *voiceless*,
which was probably only distinctive for noncontinuants in

PIE, has become distinctive for sibilants as well in Slavic because of the introduction of z in almost all consonantal contexts as a reflex of $*\acute{g}$.

Another example of rephonologization from the history of Slavic exemplifies an instance of rephonologization affecting the system of correlations. The development of Slavic g in certain dialects as γ is the case in point. Slavic inherits from Pre-Slavic a voicing opposition in the system of stop conso- nants (p, t, k / b, d, g). There also occurs in Slavic the phoneme x, which is derived from a variety of sources historically. As a result of the change, $g > \gamma$, the voicing opposition is ex- tended to continuants—to x/γ—and k comes to be isolated with respect to the feature [voice].

Before proceeding to a discussion of phonological change as described in the framework of generative phonology, let us contrast the two similar classifications of phonological change just described. The Prague School's system fails to incorporate a way to characterize the kinds of changes that leave the system of phonological oppositions intact but that result in a reorganization of the tokens of occurrence of given phonemes in specific morphemes—the case of primary split. Such changes do affect the system of phonological structure in a language, altering the phonemic representation of forms, sometimes resulting in a general readjustment of the system of morpheme structure. On the other hand, considering the preoccupation with the issue of phonemic opposition (or con- trast) in the American structuralist school, it is not surprising that this type of change represents an important category in their taxonomy. Primary split is a change resulting in a realign- ment in the system of phonemic oppositions, and is hence a type of change considered to affect the phonemic system. It is this same preoccupation with the system of oppositions, however, that leads American structuralism to neglect certain changes that affect the system of correlations.

A system restricted to the notions merger and split cannot characterize an unconditioned change of the type Pre-Greek $u >$ Attic Greek [y] as an instance of genuine phonological change. Certainly, the phonological representation of the sound in question is different for a speaker of Pre-Greek and for his Athenian descendent. Moreover, the feature [round] has a status in the phonological system of the Attic speaker which it did not have in the earlier system. The Prague School's concern with matters of phonological correlation highlights this important type of phonological change, but it is missed in a system concerned essentially with contrasting seg-mental entities and with changes in that system of segmental contrast.

GENERATIVE PHONOLOGY

The account of phonological change developed by the gener-ative school of phonology is similarly a product of a particular theoretical viewpoint. The generative school assumes that grammars are rule-governed systems. Phonological systems are assumed to consist of a set of underlying representations incorporating all the idiosyncratic information concerning any given linguistic form. They are also assumed to consist of a set of surface representations derived from underlying forms by rules of grammar that are the formal devices used by speak-ers to make generalizations about their language.

Because of the generative grammarians' special concern with the synchronic rules of grammar, generative discussions of linguistic change have centered on those developments as-sociated with the introduction and loss of alternations. Little regard has been accorded to other types of change that alter the phonological system and phonological structure. In Robert King's book (1969), which has become the standard reference for generative historical linguistics, three major types of rule change are discussed—*rule addition, rule loss,* and *rule reor-dering.* Recently, a fourth type of rule change, *rule inversion,* has been described by Vennemann (1972). In a rule inversion, surface representations come to be reinterpreted as underlying representations, and forms consistent with the ''old'' under-lying representations come to be derived by rule.

Virtually any conditioned sound change will be accompan-ied by a rule addition, because that sound change introduces paradigmatic alternations. The rule that is added will, for the most part, be equivalent to the conditioned sound change it reflects. The sound change called Germanic umlaut, whereby V (back) > V (nonback) / ＿＿＿ C(C)V (nonback) introduces a synchronic phonological rule of the same form: V (back) → V (nonback) / ＿＿＿ C(C)V (nonback).

Rule loss, on the other hand, is generally not the result of a sound change. A standard example of rule loss is seen in Yiddish. Yiddish is a dialect closely related to Middle High German. Middle High German has inherited a rule of final devoicing whereby voiced obstruents devoice in word-final position; MHG *tage* 'days' appears as *tac* in the singular. Yiddish has lost this rule; consider Yiddish *lid* 'song' and *lider* 'songs'. It should be noted that the Yiddish innovation would traditionally be treated as an instance of leveling. Where there was once an alternation, there is no longer an alternation. Forms showing final voiceless obstruents as a result of the High German final devoicing rule retain a voiceless consonant if they are not associated with some paradigm; hence, MHG *avek* and Yiddish *avek* 'away'. The characterization of this change as rule loss highlights the effect leveling has had on the phonological system.

Similarly, rule reordering serves as a way of characterizing changes in the system of phonological rules that are associated with developments traditionally considered in terms of the morphological system. A case from German is illustrative. Subsequent to the introduction of the High German rule of final devoicing, there was a sound change in German of the form V > V̄ / ＿＿＿ C (voiced). Considering the chronology of these two sound changes we should expect derivations of the type in (5.2).

(5.2)

Stage One

Underlying form	lob	lobəs	veg	vegə
Final devoicing	lop	. . .	vek	. . .
Vowel lengthening	. . .	lo:bəs	. . .	ve:gə
Surface form	lop	lo:bəs	vek	ve:gə

German does not show an alternation between long and short

vowels in such forms, however. A long vowel appears
throughout the paradigm. It is possible to characterize this
development as a rule reordering, as in (5.3).

(5.3)
Stage Two

Underlying form	lob	lobəs	veg	vegə
Vowel lengthening	lo:b	lo:bəs	ve:g	ve:gə
Final devoicing	lo:p	. . .	ve:k	. . .
Surface form	lo:p	lo:bəs	ve:k	ve:gə

Note that, as in the case of rule loss, rule reordering is concomitant with paradigmatic leveling. In fact as a result of the
leveling out of the alternation V/V̄, it would seem unnecessary
to assume that the relevant forms continue a lexical representation with a short vowel. Without any synchronic evidence
to suggest that speakers consider [lo:p], and [ve:k] to have
underlying short vowels, it seems unnecessary to assume a
second stage derivation as in (5.3). It might be preferable to
assume that leveling has resulted in a change in the phonological shape of forms like *lob* and *veg* from /lop/ /vek/ to /lo:p/
/ve:k/.

An example of rule inversion is seen in the development of
Sanskrit velar stops discussed in chapter 3. Recall that Pre-
Indic k, g > c [tš], j [dǐ] when followed by a front vowel. After
some front vowels fall together with nonfront vowels, the
conditions on the alternations $k \sim c$ and $g \sim j$ come to appear
less natural. Consequently, there occurs a generalization of
the c alternant to all prevocalic and preconsonantal contexts.
A rule k, g > $č$, $ǰ$ / ___ + Sonorant is not a natural rule (+
here refers to a morpheme boundary). If we assume, however,
that speakers come to consider the alternants with the palatals
as the underlying forms, a more natural synchronic process
would be posited for the language:

(5.4)

$$č, ǰ > k, g / \text{\_\_\_} \left\{ \begin{matrix} \text{obstruent} \\ \# \end{matrix} \right\}.$$

Such a rule accounts for all palatal/velar alternations, and it coincides with what appear to be the native intuitions of the traditional grammarians. Note that although the endingless nominative of Sanskrit *vāk* 'voice' ends in *k*, the alternant *vāc*- is given as the citation form of the stem. This is true for all stems with palatal versus velar alternations. It appears clear that although Sanskrit palatal affricates are historically derived from velar stops, in the synchronic grammar the stops are derived from underlying palatals in morphemes where alternations occur.

Rule addition and phonetic split are equivalent notions, both referring to situations whereby morphophonemic alternations are introduced into a language. Rule loss, reordering, and inversion classify a variety of different phonological changes resulting from instances of nonphonological or phonetic plus nonphonological changes. Consequently, the explication of these phenomena represents a significant contribution both to our understanding of the ways in which synchronic phonological systems are organized and of the range of and limitations on possible phonological changes. In the taxonomies of the Prague School and American structuralism, the account of phonological restructuring resulting from nonphonological changes is restricted largely to phonemic splits (secondary split or phonologization).

It should be pointed out that many instances of change cannot be described as rule changes, and such changes are not dealt with in any detail in the generative literature. Complete mergers, for example, have no effect on the system of phonological rules. Such changes are categorized in generative phonology as primary changes, and are said simply to result from innovation. An account of the effect of historical changes on the makeup of the system of phonological oppositions appears outside the scope or concern of generative historical phonology as that discipline currently approaches issues of phonological change. There exists considerable evidence for the phonological reality of the system of distinctive phonological contrasts, and it is quite likely that this system may play an important role in the motivation of at least certain sound changes. Moreover, reference to changes in the system of contrasts is accorded an important role in the establishment of genetic relationship, language split, and other facts concerning the internal histories of language families. The failure to offer any enlightening account of this type of change is a noteworthy deficiency in the generative taxonomy for phonological change.

It is desirable and necessary that a descriptive account of phonological change attend both to changes in the phonological structure of morphemes, for which we might use the term *relexicalization,* and to changes in the makeup of the phonological system, for which we might restrict the use of the term *restructuring.* In the case of restructuring, we might distinguish between those types affecting only the phonemic inventory, such as merger, and those affecting the system of rules, such as secondary split. The former necessarily coincides with widespread relexicalization, whereas the latter may or may not. Relexicalization may occur with or, as in the case of primary split, without concomitant change in the phonemic inventory.

Such a distinction is appropriate within any framework for phonological structure. For example, in the case of a change such as Latin rhotacism, the nature of the restructuring will be different for the structural or taxonomic phonemicist than for the generative phonologist. For the structuralist, there will be a change in the phonemic shape of every form (morph) that undergoes rhotacism, hence introducing multiple lexical representations for all forms affected by the sound change. For the generativist the innovation will affect the system of rules (hence, a restructuring has taken place), *but* there will be no change in the lexical representation of forms that show the innovating alternation $s \sim r$: *genus* 'kind' (nom.) ← /génVs/; *generis* (gen.) ← /genVs-is/. (The underlying representation of the vowel of the second syllable is of no concern here.) However, it is usual that innovations resulting in a change in the system of alternations will also affect segments occurring in morphemes or in positions within morphemes, where no alternation arises. Such is the case in a form like *Valesius* becoming *Valerius* after Latin rhotacism. A structural change in the phonological shape of morphemes has occurred and might well be classified with other such changes of the same type. As has been noted, the term relexicalization seems appropriate.

RECOMMENDED READING

Hoenigswald, H. M. (1946) "Sound Change and Linguistic Structure," *Language* 22, 138-43.

Hoenigswald, H. M. (1960) *Language Change and Linguistic Reconstruction,* University of Chicago Press, Chicago, Illinois.

Jakobson, R. (1931) "Prinzipien der historischen Phonologie," *Travaux du Cercle Linguistique du Prague* 4, 227-287.

Jeffers, R. J. (1976) "Restructuring, Rephonologization and Reversion in Historical Phonology," in *Recent Developments in Historical Phonology,* J. Fisiak, ed., Mouton, The Hague.

King, R. D. (1969) *Historical Linguistics and Generative Grammar,* Prentice Hall, Englewood Cliffs, New Jersey.

King, R. D. (1973) "Rule Insertion," *Language* 49, 551-576.

Venneman, T. (1972) "Rule Inversion," *Lingua* 29, 209-242.

CHAPTER SIX
EXPLANATION IN LINGUISTIC CHANGE: THE CASE OF SOUND CHANGE

Change is the basic concern of historical linguistics, and the linguist seeks to determine which specific events of change characterize the histories of given languages and which, coincidentally, enlighten our understanding of synchronic structural systems. Based on a knowledge of the histories of many languages, typologies of change can also be established, as discussed in chapters 1 and 4. As we have seen in chapters 2 and 3, methods have been developed to permit the reconstruction of lost stages in the histories of languages and language families so as to offer greater scope to the investigation of the phenomenon of language change. Historical linguistic research does not, however, stop with an account of the facts of language change. Linguistics as a science is centrally concerned with the explanation of linguistic phenomena. Historical linguistics must, in turn, seek an explanation (or, more likely, explanations) for the phenomena of linguistic change. In this chapter we will consider the case of sound change as an example of attempts at explanation by historical linguists.

In preceding chapters we have treated sound change as a fact of language history, which it is. We have not, however, considered the issues associated with a theory of sound change. What are the internal motivations that serve to activate changes in the inventory of sounds speakers use from generation to generation? What are the mechanisms through which such changes are realized? Why does a particular sound change occur at a given point in the history of a language? These and others are questions of concern to the historical linguist. Unfortunately, no universally accepted explanations for the problems these questions pose have yet been found. This is not to say that linguists have disregarded these issues. On the contrary, explanations of sound change (or, at least, of various aspects of sound change) have long been sought, and, especially in the last thirty years, many important insights have been achieved. We will present here a representative survey of discussions on sound change, with some attempts at critical comment and synthesis as we proceed. The following paragraphs are not meant as an exhaustive history of the discussion of the question of sound change. We hope, rather, to offer instructive examples of the ways in which selected scholars have approached an important and basic theoretical issue of historical linguistics.

NEOGRAMMARIAN THEORIES

The Neogrammarians were a group of young scholars working at Leipzig in the second half of the nineteenth century, the most notable being Karl Brugmann and Hermann Osthoff. Much of what they suggested actually represented accepted practice on the part of many scholars of the period, but they were the first to make explicit the demand that the investigation of linguistic phenomena must be guided by basic assumptions about the nature of the phenomena themselves. For the Neogrammarians the basic assumption to be made about sound change was, of course, that it is absolutely regular. In modern terms, it might be said that the regularity hypothesis was the Neogrammarian theory of sound change.

Many earlier scholars had accepted the notion of sporadic sound change and were willing to presume genetic ties on the basis of widespread phonetic similarity in the lexicons of languages. For the Neogrammarians such an assumption disregarded the widespread regularity of phonetic correspondence that was to be noted in related languages. That regularity demanded explanation. The acceptance of sporadic sound change was, moreover, an admittance that sound change was not amenable to rigorous scientific investigation. The regularity hypothesis eliminated both problems. If by its very nature sound change was exceptionless under statable phonetic conditions, regular phonetic correspondences in related languages would be the natural, in fact the only possible, result. Furthermore, if the regularity hypothesis was to serve as the basic axiom, the guiding principle, for linguistic investigation, exceptions to otherwise regular correspondences could not be tolerated. "There must," as Karl Verner put it in 1877, "be a rule for exceptions to a rule."

Although in the early Neogrammarian writings no explicit statement is made concerning the causes of sound change, it is apparent that for many Neogrammarian scholars, the very presence of a sound in a given syntagmatic phonetic environment served as sufficient motivation for and explanation of the occurrence of most types of sound change. In cases of unconditioned sound change, however, no contextual motivation (at least, in the Neogrammarian sense) is available, and even for conditioned sound changes many questions arise. Why does a given phonetic context prompt change in one instance and not in another? Why don't identical changes take place whenever and wherever identical conditions obtain?

In his *Prinzipien der Sprachgeschichte* Hermann Paul presented a compendium of Neogrammarian theoretical views. In his attempt to bring together many of the assumptions that guided historical linguistic research in the later nineteenth century, Paul offers the most straightforward and complete statement of Neogrammarian thinking to have appeared. With respect to sound change, he makes explicit the acceptance of an articulatory motivation (ease of articulation).

He does not, however, view sound change to be a purely physical phenomenon. He emphasizes the psychological relation that holds between sounds, noting, for example, that regressive assimilation is not simply a purely physiological (mechanical) event. For Paul, the "idea" of the sound yet to be uttered affects the articulation of the preceding segment. The conditions for sound change are physiological, and the event depends on physiological factors, but the process resulting in sound change is, in essence, a psychological phenomenon. The conviction that sound change is a purely mechanistic phenomenon is to be associated with the American structuralist school, especially that school's most notable figure, Leonard Bloomfield.

STRUCTURALIST THEORIES OF LANGUAGE CHANGE

It was Bloomfield's desire to place linguistics among the sciences. Hence, for linguistics to be scientific, linguistic investigation would have to be impersonal, nonintuitive, mechanical, and strictly formal. Meaning, frequency of occurrence, and other nonformal features of language were largely to be ignored. It is not surprising, then, that the basic assumptions of the Neogrammarians were deemed by Bloomfield an ideal basis for structuralist historical phonology. The total rejection of sporadic events of change and the mechanical character of what he considered purely physical (phonetic) contexts as an explanation for sound change proved entirely appropriate to Bloomfield's antimentalist approach to science. Bloomfield was convinced that sound change is simply the result of an alteration in speakers' habits of articulatory movement, and that nonphonetic factors could never prove relevant to sound change. Yet, although he deplored the acceptance of sporadic sound change, he admitted the sporadic occurrences of historically aberrant forms. His complaint against those of his predecessors and contemporaries who supported a notion of sporadic sound change was against their disregard for explanation. Why should speakers treat individual items of the lexicon in an exceptional manner? It should be noted, however, that he did allow the possibility that further refinements in linguistic theory might lead to an even better correlation of the facts (see Bloomfield, 1933, p. 355) than did the assumptions of the Neogrammarian school. For Bloomfield the Neogrammarian hypothesis was the best working hypothesis.

Bloomfield's remarks on sound change do, of course, go beyond a simple defense of Neogrammarian tenets as he viewed them. He asserts, for example, that sound change as a dynamic phenomenon cannot be studied. The term sound change is for him a retrospective label; it refers to a hypothesis necessitated by the data of linguistic comparison and reconstruction. We can only know of the existence of sound change through the evidence of cognates.

The importance of synchronic linguistics and structuralism

in early twentieth-century linguistic thought is also apparent
in Bloomfield's approach to the study of sound change. Since
phonemes are the structural entities of which synchronic phonological systems are composed, the study of sound change
becomes, for structural linguistics, the study of phonemic
change. A change is linguistically relevant only insofar as it
affects the structural system of a language. Bloomfield's dic-
tum "Phonemes change," highlights the attitude that historical
linguistics is the study of movement from one synchronic
system to another, later and structurally different synchronic
system. Hence, structuralist historical phonology was basically taxonomic, on the model of structuralist synchronic phonology.

A later structuralist, Charles Hockett, attempted to offer an
explicit model to describe and hence to explain this mechanical
event of sound change. Hockett attempts to explain sound
change in terms of random free variation in the actual articulation of phonemes. Sound change is associated with the
speech habits of an individual, since each speaker is constantly
attempting to hit an articulatory target (a *frequency maximum*). The speaker rarely hits the target but the range of
possible articulations is limited (the *expectancy distribution*).
Because the target is frequently "missed," the expectancy
distribution, and hence the frequency maximum, may drift
within phonological space. New targets are established, and
phonemic change takes place.

Hockett gives an array of extralinguistic reasons for speakers' failure to maintain a given frequency maximum, including
moisture in the vocal tract, wax or dirt in the ears, and general
sloppiness. He argues, moreover, that lackadaisical articulation is possible because of the manifest redundancy of language. Hockett assumes that sound change is totally irrelevant
to the speakers of a language and that they are totally oblivious
to it. Sound change is only relevant to the linguist, and then
only when some structural change has resulted. Yet, unlike
Bloomfield, Hockett considers subphonemic phonetic wandering to have theoretical importance since it serves as an
explanation for the *actuation* of potentially significant struc-

tural change. Actuation refers to the initiation of the event of change and the factors which cause the initiation of change.

The position associated with Hockett is plagued with explanatory deficiencies, some of which will become apparent in the continuing discussion, but two of which we will note here. First, the Hockett model disregards the fact that sound change, including unconditioned sound change, has direction, particularly within a specific linguistic system. Why, for example, would certain unconditioned sound shifts, such as stop > continuant, always operate in the same direction if Hockett's appeal to phonetic wandering represents a full explanation of sound change? Secondly, as the foremost antimentalist linguist of the post-Bloomfieldian era, how does Hockett explain the target at which speakers continually aim? If speakers have knowledge of something that they are continually trying to reproduce, we must ask where that knowledge is stored.

PRAGUE SCHOOL EXPLANATIONS

Although Hockett attempts to offer a model for the event of sound change, it is clear that American structuralist phonologists disregarded some of the same crucial questions the Neogrammarians failed to pose. Why do only certain sound changes occur to the exclusion of others, and why at one time rather than any other? Among the earliest attempts to answer these questions was one made by a linguist identified with the Prague School of structuralist phonology, André Martinet. For Prague School linguists everything concerning language must be considered from the point of view of function. Functional concerns directed another Prague School scholar, Roman Jakobson, in his development of a typology for phonological change. The descriptive linguist must concern himself with questions of function, asking What is the function of language? (to communicate), or What is the function of linguistic forms? (to distinguish meaning). Similarly the historical linguist asks: What is the function of linguistic change? For conditioned sound change, Paul's "ease of articulation" had become the widely accepted answer to that question. However, little attention beyond vague discussions of phonetic wandering had been given as explanation of unconditioned sound change in the nineteenth century and early twentieth century. Martinet addressed the problem of unconditioned sound change from the expected functionalist perspective.

Martinet asked, for example, the following question. If it is the function of phonemes to keep morphemes distinct, how can complete mergers occur? He suggests the following hypothesis as one possible answer. If a given phonemic distinction develops a low *functional yield*—that is, if very few morphemes are differentiated by the occurrence of one or the other of two phonemes—a merger will be of little consequence to the system and may occur without significant disruption to communication. Many factors must be taken into account in determining the functional yield for any particular phonemic distinction. The English contrast between θ and ð, for example, distinguishes very few morphemes. Yet these phonemes exhibit only one manifestation of a very important phonological correlation in English, voiced versus unvoiced, a fact that may well play a role in maintaining the stability of that distinction.

It is often the case that several related unconditioned sound changes affect a subsystem of a language's phonological system almost simultaneously. Martinet notes that languages seem to prefer symmetrical phonological systems (most contemporary linguists would speak in terms of more natural phonological systems), and he suggests that the function of, at least, some sound shifts is to bring symmetry (more naturalness) into an otherwise asymmetrical (less natural) system. In his discussions of sound shift, Martinet distinguishes between *push chains* and *drag chains*. If speakers' articulation of some phoneme /x/ begins to encroach upon the phonological space associated with some other phoneme /y/, then /y/ may begin to undergo a shift in the same direction as /x/ so that merger may be avoided. This is a push chain. On the other hand, if there exists a gap (an asymmetry) in the phonological system of a language, and if the articulation of some phoneme is altered so as to fill that gap, a drag chain may develop.

Martinet suggests such a drag chain reaction for a certain
Provençal dialect of Hauteville.

The dialect in question offers a classic example of a neatly
symmetrical vowel system. The vowel phonemes are given in
(6.1). At an earlier time the vowel inventory for this same
dialect was as given in (6.2).

(6.1)

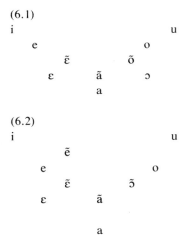

(6.2)
i   u
                    ẽ
        e   o
                    ɛ̃   õ
        ɛ   ã

                        a

The complex set of sound changes that produces (6.1) is as
follows: $a > ɔ$ $ɛ̄ > a$; $ɛ̄ > ɛ$; $ẽ > ɛ̄$. Martinet suggests that the
asymmetry in (6.2) (the lack of a three-way back vowel distinction that would mirror the three-way front vowel distinction) motivated an initial shift of $a > ɔ$, resulting in a drag
chain that might be characterized as follows: $ɔ < a < ɛ < ɛ̄$
$< ẽ$.

Despite Martinet's interesting and important hypotheses
concerning the mechanisms and explanations of certain sound
shifts, there remains a problem that he admits, namely, that
most of his functional explanations refer to sound changes that
are themselves secondary. In the case of a push chain, for
example, what activates the initial tendency toward encroachment? In the case of a drag chain, if phonological systems
tend toward symmetry, how might there arise the gaps that
the sound shift serves to repair?

GENERATIVE EXPLANATIONS

Just as Martinet and other European structuralists have sought explanations for linguistic change through a consideration of the internal structures of languages, so too have many scholars associated with the generative school of phonology. For most early generativists, most notably Paul Postal in *Aspects of Phonological Theory* (1968), sound change per se does not represent a particular type of linguistic change; it is merely one manifestation of *grammar change*. Grammar change is reflected in an alteration in the underlying representation of linguistic forms and/or a change in the system of rules relating underlying (semantic) structures to surface (phonetic) structures.

Postal laments that most attempts to explain sound change before the advent of generative phonology were based on performance (on ease of articulation, for example). He asserts that change must affect the internalized, abstract system, and that consequently surface, superficial (phonetic) factors play no special role. On the one hand, Postal supports the Neogrammarian hypothesis of regular sound change, noting that if linguistic changes are regarded as rule changes or rule additions then all forms meeting the structural description of a rule will change in accordance with alterations in the system of rules that define a grammar; on the other hand, he breaks with the Neogrammarian assumption that all regular sound change is phonetically conditioned. If we allow morphophonemic and morphological conditions (for that matter, even syntactic conditions) for sound changes, then analogy, leveling, and other processes become potentially formalizable in a manner like that associated with phonetically conditioned sound changes. We will return to this issue shortly, but let us first consider what is perhaps the most significant contribution in the generativist discussion of linguistic change.

Generative scholars have played an important part in highlighting the role of acquisition of language in linguistic change. Postal, Paul Kiparsky (1968), Robert King (1969), and others have pointed out that innovations in adult grammars in the form of rule additions may often result in situations whereby children acquiring language are confronted with data for which a grammar might be constructed that is simpler than the one their parents' generation has internalized and adjusted. The schema in figure 6.1, adapted from King and from Klima (1965)

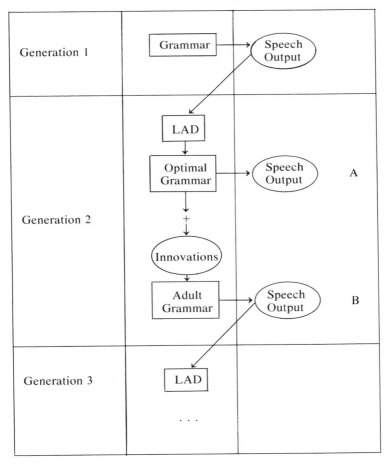

Figure 6.1   A model of linguistic change (based on Klima 1965 and King 1969).

portrays this model for linguistic change. A second suggested mechanism associated with language acquisition for language change is *imperfect learning*. This hypothesis asserts that children may not learn the grammar of their elders in all details. A highly constrained rule may be generalized, or a difficult rule may fail to be learned. These developments would, of course, result in language change.

As noted in chapter 5, the generative model itself defines and delimits the ways in which generative scholars view phonological change. Generative phonologists have for the most part equated phonological change (change in the grammatical, in particular the phonological, system) with sound change (changes in the articulation of segments). They share this prejudice with their predecessors of the American structuralist school. Sound change was explained for some, Postal most notably, if it could be described in terms of formalizable grammar changes. However, the statement that at some time X, the grammar of language A did not include some rule, but that at time X' a given rule is added to the grammar of A explains little. It is a formal statement of a historical fact; it is a *diachronic correspondence*, a term more general than the term phonetic correspondence. It is a new, and perhaps more complete version of a statement of the form $x > y$. However, as noted in chapter 5, certain important changes are not even statable in terms of changes in the system of rules.

Postal and some other generative linguists seemed not concerned with certain issues of crucial concern to most historical linguists. For him the only explanation for the occurrence of rule alterations is to be found in the common human tendency toward stylistic variation. This is no more enlightening than Hockett's notions of random variation. Postal, like Hockett, seems to disregard the fact that change is not unrestricted. It is directional, and its directionality is to some extent predictable. If sound change is equivalent to alterations in the form of phonological rules, then any alterations of feature specification, conditions, or orderings should be possible sound changes. This is clearly not the case. Hence, even if we choose to describe sound change (or some sound changes) in terms of changes in the system of phonological rules, it remains to be determined what the constraints on rule change are, and why such constraints exist.

There have been a number of attempts to determine the conditions under which rule changes might occur. Kiparsky (1968) theorized that rule reordering is motivated by a tendency for rules to apply to the greatest possible number of forms. If one of the two possible orderings for any pair of rules results in a broader application for one of those rules, that ordering is said to be the less marked of the two. Kiparsky claimed that rules tend to reorder so as to apply in the least marked order.

Any two rules that potentially apply to the same forms may show any one of four possible relationships. Given two rules A and B, A then B is a *feeding* order if the output of A produces a form to which B will apply. If the operation of A alters forms to which B might otherwise apply, then A is said to *bleed* B. If A, then B is a feeding order but B does not bleed A, then B–A is termed a *counter-feeding* order. Similarly, if A, then B is a bleeding order, but B does not feed A, then B–A is a *counter-bleeding* relationship. Hence, not only bleeding order, but counter-feeding order is more marked than feeding order, and bleeding order is more marked than counter-bleeding and feeding order.

One of the earliest and perhaps most well known of the alleged examples of a change explainable by reference to a shift from a marked to a less marked order of rules was offered by Kiparsky. In most Finnish dialects there is a rule changing geminate midvowels to diphthongs (*ee, oo > ie, uo*) preceding a rule by which intervocalic voiced continuants are deleted. Hence, earlier forms of the shape **vee* 'take' and **teɣe* 'to do' become *vie* and *tee*, respectively, in Standard Finnish, as shown in (6.3). However, in the Sarvelian dialect of Finnish **vee* and **teɣe* give *vie* and *tie*. Kiparsky contended that this difference reflects an innovation to be explained in terms of rule reordering. See (6.4).

(6.3)

	vee	teɣe
Diphthongization	vie	. . .
Loss of medial continuant	. . .	tee
Surface forms	vie	tee

(6.4)

	vee	teɣe
Loss of medial continuant	. . .	tee
Diphthongization	vie	tie

Although the situation in the two dialects demonstrates neatly the difference between a counter-feeding and a feeding relationship, further review of the facts of language history showed that the situation in Sarvelian was due to rule diffusion rather than rule reordering; that is, diphthongization spread to the Sarvelian dialect only after the loss of intervocalic voiced continuants was complete. Rather than establishing an explanation for rule reordering as a dynamic process of linguistic change, the Finnish example demonstrates how wavelike developments might account for different orderings in related dialects.

Two of the many counterexamples to the claim that markedness motivates rule reordering are the following:

(6.5)

Early English	dæg	dæges	dægas
Devoicing	dæx	. . .	. . .
Vocalization	. . .	dæjes	. . .
Later OE	dæg	dæges	dægas
Vocalization	dæj	dæjes	. . .
Devoicing	. . .	. . .	. . .

(6.6) Old English

Historical order	tæljan	tæliþ
Consonant Gemination	tælljan	. . .
Breaking	tæalljan	. . .
Umlaut	tielljan	teliþ
j-Deletion	tiellan	. . .

Synchronic order	tæljan	tæliþ
Breaking	. . .	. . .
Consonant Gemination	tælljan	. . .
Umlaut	telljan	teliþ
j-Deletion	tellan	. . .

Note that Vocalization bleeds Devoicing in example (6.5) and that in example (6.6) Breaking then Consonant Gemination is a counter-feeding order, while the historical order for these rules is a feeding order. Notice, however, that in both cases the result of changes is paradigmatic regularity. What we encounter here seem to be cases of what traditionally has been termed leveling. If rule reordering is indeed involved in developments of the type described in (6.5) and (6.6), that reordering is apparently motivated by the tendency to simplify the surface manifestation of morphemes, so that many allomorphs are replaced by a single phonetic representation for a morpheme.

NATURAL PHONOLOGY

Like the Prague functionalists, naturalists, in particular natural phonologists like David Stampe (1969), are concerned with the explanation of language change. Natural phonology seeks to account for all types of genuine sound change in a unified way. It is suggested that all human beings come to the language acquisition process with a set of innate processes that begin to operate from the commencement of speech behavior. In order that language might function to distinguish meaning, complex phonological systems have been developed in natural language. Consequently the child must suppress or order many of his natural articulatory tendencies in order to learn the phonological system. Sound change will take place, then, when speakers fail to suppress or properly order some natural process. A conditioned sound change, for example, is not to be viewed as *x* becoming *y* in the environment preceding Q, but as *x* ceasing to fail to become *y* in the environment preceding Q.

Although natural phonology offers an innovative approach

to the old problem of sound change, certain fundamental and long-standing questions remain. Just as we might ask the Neogrammarian, why $x > y$ / _____ Q in language A but not in language B, at time T_1 but not at time T_2, we might ask the natural phonologist what kinds of conditions must obtain before a process that has consistently been suppressed, suddenly or gradually ceases to be suppressed. Or why does x cease to fail to become y / _____ Q in language A but not in language B, at time T_1 but not at time T_2? Although natural phonology attempts to revise traditional assumptions about the very nature of the mechanisms operating in language change, the old problems of actuation are far from solved.

SOCIAL MOTIVATIONS FOR SOUND CHANGE

A particularly innovative, sociolinguistic approach to the explanation of sound change (and for that matter all sorts of linguistic change) has been pursued since the middle 1960s by a group of scholars, most notably William Labov, who claim that the only way to come to an understanding of language change is to study it in progress. Recall Bloomfield's claim that such a study would be impossible. Labov points out that twentieth-century linguists have studied language as if it were a homogeneous entity, whereas in actuality it is quite heterogeneous. Nondistinctive variation has not been a traditional concern of the historical linguist. The fact that the grammars of individual speakers incorporate many variables of pronunciation and structure is nowhere given attention in the historical linguistic literature.

Labov sees grammars as consisting of rules of the type $/x/ \rightarrow \langle a,b \rangle$ which abbreviates the following: $/x/ \rightarrow$ [a] in social context A; $/x/ \rightarrow$ [b] in social context B. Language change occurs, it is claimed, when one of these variables, as a consequence of its association with some positive social index, comes to be favored over the other(s) (one of which was formerly the favored representation). Or it may occur when one variable becomes stigmatized and is hence eliminated. Languages do not manifest variables for all constructs at all

times, however, and the set of variables for any definable
construct differs among languages and at various points in the
history of any language. Although the Labovian scenario
speaks with insight to the *transition problem* (the explication
of the social mechanisms that operate in the transition from
one system to another), the actuation problem again goes
unaddressed. Particular sets of variables arise at particular
points in the history of a language. It remains necessary to
determine why and how certain variable representations arise
at particular points in time in any given language.

DIALECTOLOGY

Most scholars concerned with change in the phonological
structure of words have concentrated on the uniformity of
developments, and some have emphasized the individual histories of words, addressing themselves to the issue of why
sound change is *not* always regular. During the late nineteenth
and early twentieth centuries, specialists in dialectology,
among them Jules Gilliéron and Hugo Schuchardt, called attention to the fact that every word has its own history. Exceptions to regular sound change do occur in individual words
due to idiosyncratic treatment by speakers. It was the asser-
tion of the dialectologists that it is only through the study of
the detailed history of each word in a language or dialect that
changes in the phonological structure of words can be genuinely understood.

LEXICAL DIFFUSION

Among modern students of sound change, proponents of the
theory of *lexical diffusion,* such as William S-Y. Wang and
Matthew Chen, show a similar interest in the explanation of
why sound change is not always regular in its ultimate effect
on language. The theory of lexical diffusion assumes that
sound change is phonetically abrupt, but lexically gradual, that
is to say that changes of the form $x > y$ begin in one group or
category of words and gradually spread through the lexicon;
sound change does not, according to the theory, affect all

morphemes simultaneously. If sound change is indeed lexically gradual, time would be more important than traditionally assumed, and competing sound changes may intersect in the course of the history of the language.

Suppose a language L experiences a lexically gradual sound change of the form $t > d$ / V _____ V. At some point there will be some tokens of t derived from $*t$ intervocalically, and some tokens of $d < *t$ in the same environment. Suppose then that a second sound change affects L of the form $d > ð$ / V _____ V, and that this development is complete before the first has spread through the lexicon. A very complex set of reflexes might result. There would ultimately be intervocalic ð from $*t$ (via d) and from $*d$, and intervocalic d from $*t$ in words not affected by $d > ð$ / V _____ V at the time of the operation of $t > d$ / V _____ V.

The theory of lexical diffusion is not unreasonable, but it is surprising that few supporting examples have been noticed in the histories of segmental sounds in well-attested and long-studied languages. Most examples put forth by proponents of the theory have come from the history of tone systems, particularly in Chinese.

MORPHOPHONEMIC AND MORPHOLOGICAL CHANGE

In the next chapter, some of the rare attempts to explain syntactic change will be considered. A brief remark on the explanation of morphophonemic and morphological change is appropriate before concluding this chapter. It will be recalled from chapter 4 that most instances of change in morphological systems are closely linked with sound changes. It is generally the case that some sound change, usually a conditioned sound change, introduces a complication in some (or some set of) morphological or grammatical paradigms. The result is a morphological system that may be considered more complex from the point of view of perception and that of learnability. Where a morpheme formerly had a single phonetic representation, where morpheme types once had one or a few canonical shapes, where morphological grammatical categories once showed one or a few structural patterns, sound change introduces multiple allomorphs, variety in the phonological shape of morphemes, and diversity in the formal pattern of grammar. As a consequence of such developments, linguistic relations apparently become more difficult to perceive and to learn. A need arises to bring greater uniformity to the forms and patterns of morphemes in order to facilitate perceiving and learning the formal relationships which obtain between them. Changes like leveling and analogy begin to operate to bring about this uniformity, and language continues to change in a cyclic fashion, alternating between the development and reduction of complexity.

RECOMMENDED READING

Anderson, H. (1973) "Abductive and Deductive Change," *Language* 49.4, 765–794.

Bloomfield, L. (1933) *Language*, Holt, Rinehart and Winston, New York, chapter 19.

Chen, M. and W. S.-Y. Wang (1975) "Sound Change: Actuation and Implementation," *Language* 51, 255–281.

Hockett, C. F. (1965) "Sound Change," *Language* 41, 185–215.

Kiparsky, P. (1968) "Linguistic Universals and Linguistic Change," in *Universals in Linguistic Theory*, E. Bach and R. Harms, eds., Holt, Rinehart and Winston, New York.

Labov, W. (1972) *Sociolinguistic Patterns*, University of Pennsylvania Press, Philadelphia, Pennsylvania, chapters 7–9.

Martinet, A. (1952) "Function, Structure, and Sound Change," *Word* 8, 1–32.

Paul, H. (1920) *Prinzipien der Sprachgeschichte*, 5th ed., Niemeyer, Halle.

Postal, P. M. (1968) *Aspects of Phonological Theory*. Harper and Row, New York, part II, pp. 231–326.

Stampe, D. (1973) "The Acquisition of Phonetic Representation," *CLS* 5, 443–454.

Vennemann, T. (1972) "Rule Inversion," *Lingua* 29, 209–242.

Wang, W. S.-Y. (1969) "Competing Changes as a Cause of Residue," *Language* 45, 9–25.

Weinreich, U., M. Herzog, and W. Labov (1968) "Empirical Foundations for a Theory of Language Change," in *Directions for Historical Linguistics,* W. Lehmann and Y. Malkiel, eds., University of Texas Press, Austin, Texas.

CHAPTER SEVEN
SYNTACTIC CHANGE

Syntax is the term linguists use to refer to the sets of patterns by which morphemes are organized into sentences. In this chapter we will be concerned with the description and explanation of changes in sentence patterns. From the outset it must be noted that the study of syntactic change has not received the same degree of attention as has the study of sound change and change in morphological systems. In fact, syntactic change is an issue hardly discussed in the traditional literature, and has often been totally disregarded in both general textbooks on historical linguistics and handbooks concerned with the histories of specific languages. Where syntax has been considered at all, the discussion has usually been restricted to a description of the semantic contexts in which particular grammatical forms are used. A list of the situations in which particular case forms might occur would be an example. For many nineteenth- and early twentieth-century scholars, historical morphology was equated with historical syntax. Consequently, there has been a dearth of research concerning the mechanisms through which syntactic patterns are replaced through time.

As might be expected, syntax has also been widely neglected by scholars concerned with linguistic reconstruction. Within traditional studies of Indo-European, for example, early scholars reconstructed PIE sentence structures virtually identical to those of Sanskrit, the language long considered the most archaic of Indo-European languages. The following ``reconstructed Indo-European fable`` by August Schleicher and the version by H. Hirt, which has modifications for the effects of the sound changes that have affected Sanskrit, both exemplify early methods of syntactic reconstruction. Schleicher's fable, published in 1868, is as follows:

Eine Fabel in indogermanischer Ursprache.

Avis akvāsas ka.

avis, jasmin varnā na ā ast, dadarka akvams, tam, vāgham garum vaghantam, tam, bhāram magham, tam, manum āku bharantam.

avis akvabhjams ā vavakat: kard aghnutai mai vidanti manum akvams agantam.

Akvāsas ā vavakant: krudhi avai, kard aghnutai vividvant-svas: manus patis varnām avisāms karnauti svabhjam gharman vastram avibhjams ka varnā na asti.

Tat kukruvants avis agram ā bhugat.

Hirt's modified version of this "reconstruction," published in 1938, is somewhat different:

owis ek'wōses-kᵂe.

owis, jesmin wƀlǝnā ne ēst, dedork'e ek'wons, tom, woghom gᵂƀrum weghontm̥, tom, bhorom megam, tom, gh'ƀmonm ōk'u bherontm. owis ek'womos ewƀwekᵂet: k'ērd aghnutai moi widontei gh'ƀmonm ek'wons ag'ontm̥. ek'wōses ewƀwekᵂont: k'ludhi, owei!, k'ērd aghnutai vidonlmos: gh'ƀmo, potis, wƀlǝnām owjôm kᵂr̥neuti sebhoi ghᵂermom westrom; owimos-kᵂe wƀlǝnā ne esti. Tod k'ek'ruwos owis ag'rom ebhuget.

And here is an English translation of the fable:

(A) sheep and horses

(A) sheep on which (there) was no wool (= a shorn sheep) saw horses, (the one) drawing (a) heavy wagon, (the one) (a) great burden, (the one) carrying a human quickly.

(The) sheep said to (the) horses: (My) heart feels anguish seeing (the) man driving (the) horses.

(The) horses said: listen, sheep, (the) heart feels anguish having seen (the) man, (the) master make (the) wool of sheep into warm clothes (for himself) and (there) is no wool for the sheep.

Having heard that (the) sheep turned away into (the) field.

With a few important exceptions, for decades the study of syntactic change and reconstruction received little attention beyond these unfortunate exercises. The central position attained by syntax within the field of linguistics since the late 1950s reawakened interest in the subject, influencing the direction of historical linguistic research. Moreover, many psycholinguists and scholars concerned with language universals have turned their attention to phenomena associated with syntactic change, and historical syntax has come to be considered widely as an area of primary research interest. In this chapter we will first discuss some of the diverse issues that have recently been raised concerning syntactic change. Then we will consider the problem and process of syntactic reconstruction. Because reconstruction is such an important tool in the investigation of language change, the elaboration and refinement of methods to be used in syntactic reconstruction is a crucial concern of historical linguistics.

It is important to establish what we might mean when we talk about syntactic change. According to one of the most widely used models of synchronic syntax, syntactic systems can be described as systems for mapping semantic structures into surface structures by means of transformations. Since semantic structures are in large part universal, syntactic change is, at once, change in surface structures and change in the system of transformations by which surface structures are derived.

Assume that in the course of its history a language L replaces sentences of type (a) with sentences of type (b).

(7.1)
a. I come for the giving of gifts.   (L_1)
b. I come to give gifts.   (L_2)

A nominal complement in (7.1a) has been replaced by what is generally termed an infinitival complement in (7.1b). No change in the semantic representation has taken place, however. For both sentences there exists a unique remote structure of a form something like [*I come*] [*I give gifts*]. The linear surface syntactic pattern has changed, as have, apparently, the transformation(s) whereby a surface structure is derived from the semantic structure these two sentences share.

The history and prehistory of most of the propositions that include infinitives in the IE languages exemplify an actual development like that just described. In Sanskrit, for example, constructions like that in (7.2a), which occur in the more archaic verses of the Rig Veda (the most ancient and linguist-

ically archaic Sanskrit text) are replaced by constructions like
that in (7.2b) in later hymns.

(7.2)

a. sa gamad indro . . . ̇ vasūnām . . . dātum
                ↑ (gen. pl.)
    come Indra   wealth   giving

'May Indra come for the giving of wealth.'

b. etavad . . . ūṣas tvam bhuya vā dātum . . . arhasi
   (acc. sg.)   (acc. sg.)
   so much Usas you more or to give   be able

'You, Usas, are able to give so much or more.'

In (7.2b) the object *vasūnām* 'wealth' of the underlying verb
dā 'give' is in the genitive case, the surface form expected of
the nominal object of a verbal noun in an IE language. The
morphological interpretation of *dātum* is nominal, that is, *dā*
(stem) *-tu* (nominal derivational suffix) + *m* (acc. sg.), as it
would have been in PIE. In (7.2b) the objects of *dātum* are in
the accusative case, the surface form expected for direct objects of transitive verbs, and the morphological interpretation
of *dātum* has changed to *dā* (stem) + *tum* (infinitive ending).
We know that *-tum* has been reinterpreted as a new suffix
because it gradually becomes widely productive as a unitary
entity and because it comes to be affixed to verbal stems as
well as roots. This change is complete at the period of Panini's
codification of Sanskrit about 400 B.C. by which time *-tum* has
replaced the great variety of complex suffixes like *tu* + *m*
which occurred in the oldest parts of the Rig Veda. A syntactic
change has taken place in the history of Sanskrit, but it should
be emphasized that the change has affected only superficial
representations. The surface morphological analysis of the
underlying verbs of the complement sentence has changed, as
has the nature of surface syntactic relationship between the
object and its verb in the complement (the case form has
changed). Nonetheless, it is one and the same set of semantic
structures that would underlie sentences of the type exemplified in (7.2a) as would underlie complex structures like that in
(7.2b).

CHANGES IN TRANSFORMATIONAL RULES

Virtually all syntactic innovation can be described in terms of changes in the transformational rules that derive surface structure. Like phonological rules, transformations might be altered. A well-known innovation that has affected and continues to affect English syntax, the encroachment of the relative and interrogative pronoun *who* with respect to *whom* has been described by Klima (1964) as a case of transformational reordering.

In example (7.3) we give the derivation of an English sentence at a point in history when *who* and *whom* were used strictly as subject and object (including object of preposition) respectively. Example (7.4) is the derivation of the same sentence after the change whereby *who* comes to be used in object contexts if the relative or interrogative word occurs in preverbal position.

(7.3)

DERIVATION: Whom could she see?

wh she Past can see he Sg.

a. Case-Marking

$\frac{V_t}{prep}$ Pronoun $\frac{V_t}{prep}$ Pronoun Case

wh she Past can see he Case Sg.

b. *Wh*-Attachment

wh X Pronoun (Case) Number Y *wh* Pronoun (case) Number X Y

wh he Case Sg. she Past can see

c. *Wh*-Attraction

wh (Pronoun Case Number) subj Tense (V^m) Verb

wh (Pronoun Case Number) Tense (V^m) Subj Verb

wh he Case Singular Past can she see

SURFACE: Whom could she see?

(7.4)

DERIVATION: Who could she see?

a. *Wh*-Attachment

b. Case-Marking

c. *Wh*-Attraction

Although it is clear that syntactic changes can be described as transformational change, it is not at all clear and is a matter of considerable controversy whether or not innovations can be motivated in the transformational component. In the case of a transformational change, like the reordering just described, it is not sufficient simply to relate the facts. A formalization of the grammar before and after a change and an explication of the structural change in terms of the devices of formal grammar do not explain the innovation. It is necessary to ask why such an alteration in the grammar might have taken place. Recall our remarks concerning the similar and related issue of rule change in the phonological system.

The few attempts to show that explanations for syntactic change are to be found in the system of rules by which surface structures are derived have proved, at best, inconclusive. The most appealing suggestion is that transformational rules, like phonological rules, tend to be reorganized so as to apply in the least marked order, that is, in the order of maximal applicability. Most syntactic changes cannot be explained by such a principle, however, and more satisfying explanations are apparently to be sought elsewhere.

Since the transformational component has proved to be an unenlightening context in which to seek motivations for syntactic change, scholars have, in general, returned to the surface syntactic patterns themselves for insights that might lead to an explanation (or explanations) for syntactic change. A wide variety of attempts to explain changes in syntactic patterning may be classified as cases of simplification, which is the tendency for surface structures to change so as to make the semantic structure they represent more accessible to hearers. Approaches to the explanation of syntactic change that concentrate on the perceptibility and learnability of syntactic structures seek to clarify this assumed tendency.

THE ROLE OF PERCEPTUAL STRATEGIES

The transformational generative approach to the study of syntax has been concerned largely with production, with the formulation of the simplest grammar by which surface structures can be derived from deeper semantic structures. Yet, as we have noted, actual case histories do not offer evidence that there is a consistent tendency for the rules of grammar to be simplified or generalized or for some formal property of rules to be maximized. Consequently hypotheses have been put forward concerning the interaction between the systems language users employ for understanding sentences and learning sentence structures, on the one hand, and syntactic change, on the other. In particular, Bever and Langendoen (1969) have claimed that speakers make use of hierarchical sets of perceptual strategies as a means of mapping external structures onto their underlying internal structures, thus suggesting that the mechanisms by which sentences are produced do not necessarily correspond to the mechanisms by which sentences are understood. If changes in one part of the grammar serve to inhibit perceptibility elsewhere, further change may be inevitable.

Consider some perceptual strategies which might be used by listeners to determine which syntactic sequences are clauses (sequences of actor/subject + action/verb + object). Since most clauses with transitive verbs in English have the order *noun - verb - noun* (NVN), all things being equal, listeners will probably segment the flow of discourse into sequences of the type NVN NVN and interpret such sequences as clauses wherever possible. When a listener is confronted with a sentence of the type represented by (7.5), interpretation of clause structure based on a strategy of the type NVN = clause is straightforward.

(7.5)
He hit the boy Mary likes.

Sentence (7.5) has an external and an internal structure that correspond to the sequence NVN / NV. A sentence like (7.6) is more complex.

(7.6)
When he left the party became dull.

The initial approach to the interpretation of (7.6) for at least some speakers may result in the tentative assumption that *when he left the party* is an actual clause of the sentence 7.6. However, since there exists no internal structure cluster corresponding to *became dull*, such an initial interpretation must be quickly reevaluated.

Bever and Langendoen suggest that certain changes in the structure of English relative clauses might be better understood in terms of the perceptual strategies available or necessary for the interpretation of such complex sentences by hearers. The changes that have affected the structure of relative clauses as English has developed over the past millennium are many and complex. Here we will briefly consider just one change in English relative clause structure as it may relate to perceptual strategies of the type just discussed. (The actual changes affecting English relative clause structure over the past several centuries are far more intricate than suggested by the following discussion, which is highly simplified for illustrative purposes.)

An interesting difference between relative clause formation in modern English and in earlier forms of English is that modern English demands the use of the relative marker (pronoun) in sentences where a relative clause modifies a noun that follows the verb in its own clause. Hence, sentence (7.7) is ungrammatical, and only sentences like (7.8) are possible. (Note that the asterisk is used here to mark synchronically ungrammatical sentences, not reconstructed forms as is the case in other chapters of this book.)

(7.7)
*He hit the boy likes Mary.
(7.8)
He hit the boy that (who) likes Mary.

At earlier stages in the history of English, however, sentences like (7.7) did occur. Consider also that there is no period in the history of English when a relative clause modifying a noun that precedes the verb of its own clause can occur without an overt relative marker. At all periods only sentences such as (7.9) are possible, to the exclusion of sentences such as (7.10).

(7.9)

The boy who (that) likes Mary hit Paul.

(7.10)

*The boy likes Mary hit Paul.

If we recall the suggestion that hearers may comprehend
the clause structure of sentences by interpreting sequences of
NVN as clauses, we should not be surprised that sentences
like (7.7) are unacceptable in modern English, as *the boy likes
Mary* ''sounds like'' a clause. The inclusion of some relative
marker assures that the hearer will interpret the noun phrase
the boy as the object of *hit* (of course, as well as being the
underlying subject of *likes*). The necessity for a relative marker
would be less pressing in Old English, however, where case-
marking would assure the proper interpretation of each noun
in a sentence as a subject or as an object of some surface
verb. But at all stages in the history of English sentences like
(7.10) would present a problem because the first sequence of
a noun and a verb, even with the case-marking, may well be
perceived as members of the same clause, and hearers will
have been led down a garden path. Consider the following
sentence:

(7.11)

He hit the boy Mary likes.

It presents no problem to speakers of modern English, even
though case-marking has been lost, because, as we have noted,
the surface structure of the sentence (NVN / NV) corresponds
to its internal structure. It is possible then to see the change
in constraints on the deletion of relative markers in English as
resulting from the loss of case-marking and from the attendant
problems for the perception of clause membership of given
nouns or noun phrases.

SYNTACTIC ANALOGY

In chapter 4 it was pointed out that the ways speakers perceived surface formal relationships between pairs of words
often resulted in a type of change termed analogy. It is quite
likely that perceived formal relationships between pairs of

sentence types might set the stage for changes that can be considered under the rubric *syntactic analogy*.

A potential example of a syntactic analogy exists in the history of Sanskrit, where the passive voice of a transitive verb is formed by the addition of the derivational suffix *-ya* to the verbal root, so that *karoti* 'he/she does/makes', for example, becomes *karyate* 'it is done/made (by X)'. The Skt. passive construction with a *-ya* suffixed finite verb is a Skt. innovation. In related IE languages we find quite different passive constructions. However, the suffix *-ya* itself is a well-known IE formative, and is assumed to have been a marker of intransitive change of state verbs in the parent language. Consider the Skt. intransitive verb *puṣyate* 'to thrive, grow, become ripe', which clearly reflects the original meaning of the suffix *-ya*.

If *-ya* is associated with verbal roots occurring in both transitive and intransitive contexts (as happens in Sanskrit), pairs of sentences like those in (7.12) will be juxtaposed in the language.

(7.12)
a. Manu pacati   ghee
   Manu is cooking butter
b. Ghee pacyate.
   Ghee is cooking (is being cooked).

Notice that for pairs of sentences of the type given in (7.12), the object of the transitive verb in (7.12a) can commonly serve as the subject of a corresponding intransitive verb like the one in (7.12b). Consider the following sentence

(7.13)
Manu karoti   damam
Manu is building a house.

The word *damam* 'house', like *ghee* 'butter', can function as the direct object of a transitive verb. Speakers of early Sanskrit may well have used a perceived relationship between sentences of types (7.12a) and (7.12b) as a model for the innovative production of sentences like (7.14).

(7.14)
Damas karyate
A house is being built.

Just as a direct object of *pacati* can serve as a subject of
pacyate, a direct object of *karoti* comes to be used as a subject
of a newly formed *karyate*.

Note, however, that the semantics associated with the three
Sanskrit verbs discussed in this section are somewhat different. With *puṣyate*, the notion *agency* is irrelevant. With *pacyate*, an implied agent is not necessarily to be assumed.
(Indeed, a semantic shift from 'is cooking (no agent)' to 'is
being cooked (implied agent)' is surely concomitant with the
introduction of constructions with verbs like *karyate*.) With
karyate, an agent is necessarily implied, and we can speak of
this verb as a genuine passive. A perceived formal relationship
between pairs of sentence types has permitted an extension
or alteration of the semantic range of a suffix, here *-ya*, resulting in innovative and productive morphological and syntactic patterns in a language.

In the foregoing two instances of syntactic change, an understanding of developments in the syntactic system cannot
be separated from a consideration of developments in other
parts of the grammar. Changes in the constraints of English
relative clause formation are intricately tied to developments
in the phonological and morphological systems, and the developments producing passive sentences in Sanskrit simultaneously produce a new grammatical category, the passive, in
the verbal morphology of that language. Some scholars, such
as Vennemann (1974), have suggested that virtually all syntactic change is intricately tied with phonological change, emphasizing the very serious effects of phonological reduction
and phonological neutralization on inflectional endings that
mark syntactic relationships. It is possible, for example, that
the loss of a distinction between nominative and accusative
case forms of nouns due to sound changes, such as a loss of
final syllables, or a neutralization of all word-final unstressed
vowels to *ə*, might result in the stabilization of, or change

toward a word order of the type subject – verb – object (SVO),
so as maximally to distinguish nouns that are subjects from
nouns that are objects by means of position in a clause relative
to the verb.

WORD ORDER

The interesting and surprisingly complex phenomena that
might be classed as word-order changes have only in the 1970s
come under widespread scrutiny. In 1973 Greenberg pointed
out that there obtain in the languages of the world systematic
relations among a variety of linearly ordered constructions,
which are of a universal character. As a result of this discovery, considerable attention has been afforded to the fact that
relations might exist between such universals in the surface
order of major sentence constituents, on the one hand, and
processes and tendencies of syntactic change, on the other.

Among the implicational universals of linear order in sentences that have been established statistically, the following
ones are moderately secure:

(7.15)

verb + object (VO)	object + verb (OV)
preposition + object	object + postposition (or case ending)
comparative + standard	standard + comparative
noun + relative clause	relative clause + noun
noun + dependent genitive	genitive + noun
auxiliary verb + main verb	main verb + auxiliary verb (or inflectional ending)

In other words, VO order generally implies *preposition +
object* order, as opposed to *object + postposition* (or case
ending) order. There are other possibilities, but the implicational relationships demonstrated in (7.15) suffice to illustrate
the nature of the universals under consideration. The realization that languages universally tend to favor typological con-
sistency permits, at the very least, the potential for some
significant generalizations concerning the direction of syntactic change. We might predict, for example, that a shift from

VO order to OV order might entail over time a replacement of prepositions with postpositional markers or the postposing of earlier preposed relative constructions.

Despite the clear promise of incorporating typological factors in diachronic studies, explications of syntactic change in the context of word-order universals by no means present a panacea for students of diachronic syntax. Fundamental questions remain unanswered. How are word-order shifts initiated in the first place? (A possible answer already considered involves the potential relationship between phonological change and word-order change.) Also, by what mechanisms are the changes associated with typological shifts effected? Constituents do not simply jump over one another in a clause. A complex set of processes comes into play whenever typological change occurs.

SYNTACTIC RECONSTRUCTION

At the beginning of this chapter we noted that attempts at syntactic reconstruction have traditionally not held a place of prominence in diachronic studies. Here we will consider some of the difficulties involved in attempts at syntactic reconstruction and identify areas of the greatest potential success. Let us begin by examining the most valuable procedure that has been developed for phonological and lexical reconstruction, the comparative method (CM), as it relates to syntactic reconstruction.

Much of the success of CM in the reconstruction of sound systems and of the morphemes and words in which these sounds occur has been dependent on the strikingly regular character of sound change, however that regularity may arise. If two languages are related, a finite number of phones will correspond within a finite number of cognate lexical items. In a sense, the sounds of a language, as well as the morphemes and words they constitute, may be viewed as continuations of the physical features of an earlier form of that language. Of course, every generation of speakers constructs its own phonological system, and the sounds of an individual's language do not represent genetic inheritance. All things being equal, however, the nature of sound change is such that there will exist a series of one-to-one correspondences between the sounds of any set of cognate languages and the sounds of their parent. The continuum is an abstraction, but it is no less real for its abstract character. And it is this continuum that permits the viability of CM. Syntax is another matter.

In syntax there does not exist a finite set of sentences occurring in a finite set of discourses that might serve as the basis for the establishment of correspondence sets. In syntax, only patterns can be compared, and patterns, in general, do not evolve the way sounds do. There is no series of one-to-one correspondences between the syntactic patterns of a language and the syntactic patterns of that language at some earlier point in its history, as there is for the sounds of a language between any two stages in its history.

A straightforward transfer of the principles of the comparative method to the reconstruction of syntax is consequently quite difficult. The history of syntactic systems is a history of pattern replacement and reanalysis. In phonological reconstruction, when sounds do not reflect the continuous tradition that results from the operation of sound changes—for example. where forms, hence segments, have been replaced because grammatical patterns have been readjusted—CM is of no value. The results of changes in grammatical patterning must be "factored out" before a form can serve as a candidate for membership in a set of cognates upon which are based the sets of correspondences.

Despite the widespread use of the term comparative morphology in historical linguistics, we do not reconstruct any other types of grammatical patterns, such as paradigms, on the basis of CM per se. We do not, that is, unless we have exact matches. In actuality, we first use the methods of internal reconstruction to discover all those language-specific developments that have produced alterations in the paradigms of the various cognate languages in order to determine the appearance of those paradigms before those changes occurred. The result is, in general, a series of paradigm types that are

exact parallels from language to language, except for the reflexes of sound change. Where some anomaly exists in the
general identity of pattern types, reconstruction becomes
problematic. As an example, consider the problem of reconstructing a dative-instrumental plural for PIE. Some IE lan-
gauges offer evidence for an ending -*mo*, while others speak
for an ending -*bho*. Instead of reconstructing a PIE dative-
instrumental plural, we refer to dialect differentiation in the
parent. Differing patterns simply do not compare. The divergent grammatical patterns of cognate languages must be
brought into line before any reconstruction can be offered.

The few genuinely successful attempts at the so-called comparative reconstruction of syntactic patterns have, in actuality,
been extensions of the methodology just described for the
reconstruction of paradigmatic patterns. Watkins, in an important attempt to reconstruct certain aspects of IE sentence
structure (1973), made use of a modified form of CM. He uses
data drawn largely from Anatolian, specifically Hittite (Hitt.),
Vedic Sanskrit (Ved.), and Old Irish (OIr.) texts. In a brilliant
series of deductions, he shows how OIr. constructions' such
as the prefixed imperfect (as in *no bered* 'he used to bring'),
and the relative clause with verbal prefixation and phonological lenition of the initial of the finite verb (as in *in salm no
chanaim* 'the psalm that I sing'; compare the nonlimited *canaim* 'I sing') must reflect IE patterns of the following form:

(7.16)
Sentence connective (such as **no-*) ± enclitic pronoun ± relative
marker (-**yo*) ± finite verb.

Such patterns are for the most part extant in Anatolian and to
some degree in Vedic. In the precursor to the OIr sentence *in
salm no chanaim* (1) no enclitic pronoun is assumed to have
been suffixed to the original sentence connective; (2) the relative marker is assumed to have occurred, hence *nó-yo*, but
is lost via a regular Irish process whereby word-final syllables
were lost or reduced; (3) the [k] spelled *c* in *canaim* undergoes
a productive sound change of Pre-Irish (lenition), whereby
voiceless stops become fricatives (*ch* spells [χ]) intervocali-

cally, even across certain word boundaries, and (4) the loss of
-*yo* obviously postdates the lenition of *k*.

The apparently extraordinary constructions of Old Irish reflect a series of boundary reanalyses, morphosyntactic rein-
terpretations, and levelings, most of which are the ultimate
result of sound changes that had massively reductive effects
on the shape of Pre-Irish forms. In any event, the Irish patterns
per se cannot be compared with those of Hittite and Vedic
until the effects of the various sound changes, pattern reinter-
pretations, and other subsequent developments are undone.
The OIr. patterns are understood historically only in terms of
the Hitt. and Ved. patterns, which we assume to be significantly more archaic. A comparison of Hittite and Irish does
not enlighten us in any significant way with respect to the
reconstruction of PIE syntax. Rather, it helps to explicate the
internal syntactic history of Old Irish while bolstering our
assumption that the sentence structure of Old Irish's far more
ancient sisters more closely reflect the pattern of the parent
language.

We note again the basic problem to be confronted in trans-
ferring CM from phonology to syntax. In the comparison of
sounds, morphemes, and words, correspondences between
constructs that are formally different yield unique reconstructions. In the comparison of morphological and syntactic systems (paradigmatic patterns and patterns of sentence structure), there exists no correspondence that is not a correspondence of identity. Reconstruction is not possible until the
cognate languages can be shown to have or to have had patterns of morphologic and syntactic structure that are essentially identical.

Because of the problems involved in the comparison of
divergent patterns, the juxtaposition of the syntactic constructions of related languages for the purpose of historical comparison may sometimes prove meaningless. What is to be
done, for example, when related languages show a corresponding pattern for what must be considered the same syntactic
category, but some of the lexical material incorporated in that
pattern is not, itself, cognate from language to language? Sup-

pose that any number of related languages share a periphrastic construction for the perfect aspect of the form *auxiliary + nonfinite verb form,* but that the several auxiliaries are not cognate. The Sanskrit perfect periphrastic with auxiliary *kr̥* 'to do' opposed to the Hittite perfect periphrastic with *ḫark-* 'to hold' is such a case. Do we reconstruct the pattern for the parent language without forms to fill the slots, or do we disregard the pattern correspondence and assume parallel development? For both Sanskrit and Hittite, we are fortunate to have a long textual tradition, which in the case of Sanskrit informs us that the perfect periphrastic is a relatively late innovation, virtually assuring that Sanskrit and Hittite offer parallel developments. But philological evidence of this quality is seldom available, and it is more likely that decisions will have to be based solely on principles of comparative reconstruction.

An even worse situation arises when related languages share syntactic categories without cognate lexical material or corresponding syntactic patterns in the formal expression of the category. The passive in Indo-European is a notorious example. There exist almost as many formal devices for the expression of the passive as there are ancient IE dialects. But even though it is often the case that no formal comparisons are possible, can we fail to reconstruct for the parent language a grammatical category that finds expression in all or most of its descendants?

What do we do when related languages share patterns with different meanings, or when they offer patterns that of necessity defy correspondence? Related languages, for example, may exhibit *all* of the possible patterns for the major constituents of a sentence; Hittite is SOV, Germanic SVO, and Celtic VSO. What does the comparativist do with that information? In phonology the divergent reflexes, such as Hitt. *p*, Gmc. *f*, and Celtic ∅ yield some protophoneme, however we might wish to characterize it phonetically. But the divergent patterns SOV, SVO, VSO yield nothing. In cases like this, the only viable alternative would appear to be internal reconstruction. The traditional procedures associated with internal reconstruction, that is, with the derivation of synchronically aberrant patterns from consistent ones, has had significant, though limited success in syntax. (The discussion of the reconstruction of the IE' verb phrase earlier in this chapter incorporated elements of IR as well as those of CM.)

Finally, it should be noted that word-order theories of the type previously discussed may prove useful in making inferences concerning reconstructed syntactic systems. Assume, for example, that most or all of the daughter languages in a family agree with respect to order of a certain subset of phrase types and we reconstruct those for the protolanguage. In cases where identical patterns do not occur, we might reasonably infer that the languages offering patterns that are typologically consistent with those already reconstructed are more archaic and more faithfully reflect the patterns of the parent. It must be kept in mind, however, that word-order theories are hypotheses based on statistically established tendencies. These hypotheses are not without exception, and they are under constant revision as we come to understand better the role played in surface structure by grammatical concepts not necessarily dependent on the traditional categories like subject, verb, and object. Issues like topic prominence versus subject prominence in languages and like ergativity versus transitivity have yet to be seriously considered in the historical linguistic literature.

RECOMMENDED READINGS

Bever, T., and D. T. Langendoen (1972) "The Interaction of Speech Perception and Grammatical Structure in the Evolution of Language," in *Linguistic Change and Generative Theory*, R. Stockwell and R. Macaulay, eds., Indiana University Press, Bloomington, Indiana.

Closs Traugott, E. (1965) "Diachronic Syntax and Generative Grammar," *Language* 41, 402–405.

Closs Traugott, E. (1969) "Toward a Grammar of Syntactic Change," *Lingua* 23, 1–27.

Greenberg, J. (1966) "Some Universals of Grammar with Particular Reference to the Order of Meaningful Elements," in *Universals of Language*, J. Greenberg, ed., 2nd ed., MIT Press, Cambridge, Massachusetts.

Givón, T. (1971) "Historical Syntax and Synchronic Morphology," *Proceedings of the 7th Regional Meeting of the Chicago Linguistic Society*, Chicago Linguistic Society, Chicago, Illinois.

Jeffers, R. J. (1976) "Syntactic Change and Syntactic Reconstruction," *Proceedings of the Second International Conference on Historical Linguistics*, W. Christie, ed., *Current Progress in Historical Linguistics*, North Holland, Amsterdam.

Klima, E. (1964) "Relatedness between Grammatical Systems," *Language* 40, 1–20.

Klima, E. (1965) *Studies in Diachronic Transformational Syntax*, unpublished dissertation, Harvard University, Cambridge, Massachusetts.

Lehmann, W. P. (1973) "A Structural Principle of Language and Its Implications," *Language* 49, 47–66.

Sapir, E. (1921) *Language*, Harcourt, Brace and World, New York, chapter 7.

Vennemann, T. (1974) "An Explanation of Drift," in *Word Order and Word Order Change*, C. Li, ed., University of Texas Press, Austin, Texas.

Watkins, C. (1962) "Indo-European Origins of the Celtic Verb," Dublin Institute of Advanced Study, Dublin.

Watkins, C. (1962) "Preliminaries to a Historical and Comparative Analysis of the Syntax of the Irish Verb," *Celtica* 6, 1–49.

CHAPTER EIGHT
LEXICAL CHANGE

At every stage in the history of any language certain words will undergo a change in meaning. We might refer to changes in the meaning of words as *lexical change*. From a structuralist point of view, the meaning of a word is determined by the set of contexts in which that word generally occurs. Lexical change can be viewed, then, as a change in the set of contexts in which a given word might occur. A more abstract characterization of lexical change emphasizes the fact that a change of reference is involved. Some lexical change is motivated by the need to characterize novel phenomena in a society or culture. Consider the history of the English word *book* as an example.

CHANGES IN MEANING OF WORDS

The reconstructed Germanic stem from which this word is derived *$\bar{o}ka$*- apparently refers to some kind of tree, possibly the beech tree. The English word *beech* is derived from a suffixed form of the same root *$b\bar{o}kyo$*-. (Note that the vowel in *b?ech* reflects both umlaut $\bar{o} > \bar{e}$ / ____ Cy . . . , and the English vowel shift $\bar{e} > \bar{\imath}$. Compare with it Latin *fagus* 'beech' and Ancient Greek *phagus*.) In ancient times it was a Germanic custom to carve inscriptions on pieces of wood. It is generally believed that *$b\bar{o}ka$*- came to be used for the pieces of wood (from the tree to which *$b\bar{o}ka$*- refers) on which inscriptional documents were composed. It then came to be generalized to the written document itself, and in turn to any written document or composition. The Modern Engish word *book*, for the modern product to which it refers, represents the current endpoint in the development of the Gmc. form *$b\bar{o}ka$*-.

For lexical change to occur, it is by no means necessary that there be a change in the nature or kinds of things to which we refer. The complex history of the English word *black* (a universal notion) demonstrates the extraordinary range within which meaning changes can occur over long periods of time.

A striking fact about the word *black* is that it is in part cognate with Slavic words for 'white', like Russian *belo* 'white' or *Byelorussia* 'White Russia'. The Proto-Indo-European root from which both English *black* and Russian *belo* are ultimately derived is **bhel*. This root occurs commonly in Indo-European languages with a suffix *-g*; hence, the IE alternants **bhelg/bhleg* are reconstructed. English *black* is derived from the suffixed form; Russian *belo* is not. The English words *bald* from Old English *ballede* 'having a white shining head' and *bleach* from OE *blæcan* 'to make white' reflect the nonsuffixed form **bhel*. Latin and Greek offer cognates with the suffix, like Lat. *fulgere* 'to flash, shine', Lat. *flagrare* 'to blaze', Lat. *flamma* (< **flag-ma*) 'flame', and Gk. *phlox* 'flame'.

It should be obvious by now that all the forms related to *black* in Slavic, Latin, Greek, and even English refer to 'shining, flashing, brightening, whitening.' The change of references in *black* is clearly extreme.

More specifically, *black* is derived from **blakaz*, the Gmc. past participle of a verb meaning 'to blaze'. The original meaning of **blakaz* would have been 'to have blazed', or 'to have burned'. As an adjective the participle would mean burned or charred. Since that which is charred is generally black, the shift of meaning seems understandable.

EXTENSION OF REFERENTS OR CONTEXTS
Lexical changes may result in an extension (generalization) of possible referents or contexts of occurrence, a reduction (specialization) of referents or contexts, or a replacement of one referent with another. Extensions of meaning frequently result from a generalization from the specific case to the class of which the specific case is a member. Consequently, proper names will come to refer to the general class of phenomena. *Bedlam*, for example, was originally the name of a specific hospital in London. The word now refers to any chaotic situation. During World War II, a Norwegian by the name of Vidkun Quisling received considerable notoriety for collaborating with the Nazis. Today, *quisling* refers to anyone who collaborates with the enemy.

In American English brand names have commonly come to be used for a given product, in general. For many speakers, *Jell-O* refers to any flavored gelatin, *Frigidaire* has replaced *refrigerator*, *Vaseline* is the common word for petroleum jelly, and a *Kleenex* is a facial tissue.

The meaning of words often becomes less narrow as a result of what might be termed *metaphorical extension*. The word *maverick* was originally a rancher's term for unbranded, loose cattle. Today, it commonly refers to an individual who does not conform to the conventions of the group, particularly in political parties. The term *broadcast*, which refers to the diffusion of radio waves through space, is a metaphorical extension of a verb for scattering seed over a field by hand. In the case of the word *broadcast*, an original extension has been followed by a restriction in reference for most speakers, who know only the more recent, metaphorical sense for the word.

Although no metaphor is involved, the history of the word *pen* is similar. The word, borrowed into English from Middle French, earlier meant 'feather' or 'quill', but was generalized to refer to the now archaic writing implements that were made of quills. Gradually, the term came to be restricted in reference to the writing implement. A subsequent generalization has resulted in the use of *pen* with reference to any writing implement that spreads ink, and terms like *ballpoint pen* are commonplace. German *Feder* has undergone the same process of extension but continues to mean 'feather' as well as 'pen.'

NARROWING CONTEXTS

Narrowing the contexts in which a word might occur seems to be a somewhat less frequent occurrence in the history of languages, but it is nonetheless a well-documented type of lexical change. The English word *skyline*, for example, originally referred to the horizon in general. Today it is used only in cases where the line of the horizon is decorated with a complex of tall buildings. The history of the word *girl* offers an interesting example of lexical restriction; its Middle English antecedent, *gurle*, refers to young people in general—both boys and girls.

REINTERPRETATIONS

Alterations in the meaning of words are sometimes caused by the reinterpretation of a form comprising more than one morpheme in terms of the semantics of one of the morphemes of which the larger word is composed. The English word *presently* traditionally meant 'at once', 'immediately', or, 'in the immediate future'. For the past several centuries *presently* has come to be synonymous with 'now', or 'at present', so that few modern day speakers of American English even recognize *presently* in the usage 'at once'.

Hopefully was formerly reserved to use as a simple adverb meaning 'in a hopeful manner', as in the sentence 'He set about the task hopefully'. In current American English vernacular *hopefully* has become a sentence adverb meaning 'it is hoped that', as in *Hopefully, a vote will be taken in the Congress before it recesses for the holiday.* The modern extension of *hopefully* must be based on the pattern of words like *clearly*, as in *Clearly a vote must be taken in the Congress before it recesses for the holiday.* The use of *hopefully* with the meaning 'it is hoped that' is unknown during most of the history of the English language.

A change of reference for one word in a language is often associated with a shift of meaning in other words that are, in some sense, semantically related. In Old English, for example, the word *mete*, which has become *meat*, referred to all forms of solid food. *Flæsc*, later *flesh*, referred to animal tissue in general. The meaning of *meat* has been restricted to the flesh of animals, and that of *flesh* has been restricted to the tissue of humans. *Foda*, later *food*, which in Old English was a word for animal fodder, has been generalized to refer to all forms of solid nourishment. It has replaced *meat* in that meaning.

IDIOMS

Idioms often result when the referent of one word in a common expression is entirely lost. That word comes to be restricted to the idiomatic expression, and is understood only in that context. Virtually everyone who speaks American English knows the idiom *to keep tabs on someone*. Most speakers, however, rarely use the term *tabs* in any other context. The Oxford English Dictionary suggests that *tabs* is an abbreviated form of *tables* or *tablets*, but even the OED is unsure of the source of this highly restricted word. Similarly, the word *kith* is virtually never used by speakers of English except in the idiomatic phrase *kith and kin*. For many English speakers the whole phrase refers to 'relatives', a usage dating from the sixteenth century. Actually, *kith* is based on a root meaning 'to know' and is derived from an OE word, *cyðð*, meaning 'acquaintances, friends'. The metaphorical extension of a word may ultimately result in the development of an idiom. In English the phrase *to field a question* has developed as a result of the extension of the baseball term 'to field' to a nonsports context. It is not unreasonable to imagine that a phrase like *to field a question* might outlive the sport that is the ultimate source of the expression.

FORMATION OF NEW WORDS

The vocabulary of a language is continually being enriched by the invention of new words. Usually, these inventions consist of lexical material already in the language. *Coinages, blends,* and *shortenings* are the most frequent instances of lexical invention. Coinage is a general term referring to the creation of new words. A blend, which may be considered a special case of coinage, results from the contraction of two existing words to make a new word incorporating certain of the semantic characteristics of each of the source words. Shortenings are abbreviated forms that often replace the older, longer version of the source word.

The generalization of a suffix or prefix is the most common mechanism by which new words are coined. The history of the English suffix *-wise* exemplifies the type of development. Before the 1940s only a few words with the suffix *-wise* were in common use (*likewise, lengthwise,* and a few others). Beginning in the 1950s this suffix began to become almost universally productive. Words like *weatherwise, healthwise,* and *timewise* are recent innovations. Parts of words that are not full morphemes are sometimes used productively in the creation of new words. *Alcoholic* clearly consists of two morphemes—*alcohol* and *-ic*. Yet, the second part of a relatively recent coinage *workaholic* 'one addicted to work', surely finds its source in *alcoholic*.

Blends are exemplified by words like *smog* (from *smoke* and *fog*); *brunch* (from *breakfast* and *lunch*); *motel* (from *motor* and *hotel*). *Flu* and *auto* (from *influenza* and *automobile* respectively), are representative of many of the shortened words that are replacing their longer versions in modern English. It should perhaps be noted that phenomena like blends and shortenings are nothing new in language. The word *dumbfound*, which first appeared in print in 1653, is apparently a blend of *dumb* and *confound*. The words *taxi* and *cab* from *taximeter cabriolet* date to 1907 and 1827, respectively.

ETYMOLOGY

It is apparent from individual histories of words that the causes of lexical change are many and varied. Almost every etymology offers a considered example of a new context in which lexical change might occur. *Etymology* is the technical term for the study of the history of words. Just as cultural change demands the invention of a new terminology for new phenomena, changes in the geographic distribution of a language may motivate alterations in the meaning of words, so that the lexicon of a language might better suit a new natural or sociocultural environment. The etymology of the IE word **laks* offers an interesting and informative case study.

In most IE languages the reflex of PIE **laks* means 'salmon'. On the basis of this correspondence of meaning linguistic paleographers concerned with the issue of the homeland of the speakers of Proto-Indo-European used the word **laks* as a piece of evidence in favor of a northeastern European homeland; salmon is commonly found in the rivers of northeastern Europe. (*Linguistic paleontology* is the study of the meaning of words in reconstructed languages for the purpose of making social, cultural, and geographic inferences about the speech communities that used those languages.) Recent archaeological research, however, has authoritatively placed the Indo-European homeland in the region of the Russian steppes—a region where the salmon is unknown. The question must be asked whether *laks* is an IE word.

This dilemma has been settled by a revision of the etymology of *laks* by Diebold (1976), which rested heavily on biological and paleobiological information. There is found today (and there has been for several millennia) a type of trout in the region of the IE homeland whose physical appearance and habits are much like those of the salmon. It seems reasonable to hypothesize that the word *laks* originally referred to that fish, and that as IE speakers moved north and west in Europe, the term came to be used for a river fish with an almost identical description, the salmon.

Words may cease to be used by a speech community due to the development of a taboo. A *taboo word* is one which has come under prohibition, usually because of the sacred status of the referent of the word in question or because of fear inspired by the referent. When taboos develop, some other word or phrase, usually a descriptive term, is generally called upon to replace the forbidden word. The Germanic word for 'bear' (and English word *bear* itself) is related to the word *brown* and originally meant 'the brown one'. The Russian word for 'bear' is *medved'*, originally meaning 'honey-eater'. Neither the Germanic nor the Slavic languages have retained a reflex of the PIE root *$r̥kso$- that has survived in the southern IE languages (as Latin *ursus*, Gk. *arktos*, Skt. *r̥kṣa-*). In Ancient Greek the word *drakōn*, which is the present participle of the verb 'to see', means 'snake'. Apparently it became taboo to refer to the snake by name, and the descriptive adjective *drakōn* 'the seeing one' replaced the earlier word for 'snake', which was completely lost from the Greek vocabulary.

ESTABLISHING COGNATES

One of the basic tenets of the comparative method is the assumption that words of similar phonetic shape and similar meaning are cognates, that is, are descendants of a common ancestor. We have seen, however, that the phonetic shape as well as the meaning of words can change over time. In deciding whether a word may properly be considered a cognate (and thus may be used for comparative reconstruction), we have to decide whether the phonetic changes as well as the semantic changes are plausible enough to justify the assumption of common origin. There are no absolute criteria for plausibility; by observing cases in which descent from a common ancestor can be documented by other means, one can develop a basis for plausibility judgments by comparing changes that are known to have occurred with those that are to be accepted if the scrutinized set of words are to be considered cognates. The question whether the phonetic shapes and meanings of two words are similar enough to consider them descendants from the same ancestor becomes particularly crucial when no alternative historical evidence is available, as is the case with languages that have no written history. There exists a method for determining degrees of relationship between languages which is based on counting the number of cognates in a particular set of vocabulary items. This method is called *glottochronology*. The accuracy of glottochronology depends basically on the linguist's ability to detect true cognates.

LEXICOSTATISTICS

Lexicostatistics is the study of vocabulary statistically for historical inference. Glottochronology is one of several possible lexicostatistic methods. As currently employed, the term glottochronology refers to the study of rate of change in languages, and the use of the rate for the estimation of time depths (the time at which two languages started on divergent development). Time depths are in turn used to provide a pattern of internal relationships within a language family. The rate of change in language means, in this context, the replacement of vocabulary items in a basic list. The originator of the method, Morris Swadesh (1950), started from the assumption that some parts of the vocabulary are much less subject to change than other parts. This basic (core) vocabulary consists of words for concepts that are assumed to be a necessary part of all human cultures. The semantic fields represented by the lexical items include pronouns, numerals, adjectives (like *big, long, small*), kinship terms (*mother, father*), living beings (*dog, louse*), body parts (*head, ear, eye*), events and objects in nature (*rain, stone, star*), and common activities (*see, hear, come, give*). There exist several versions of Swadesh's list; two of them are in common use, a 100-word list and a 200-word list.

Swadesh made several further assumptions: that the rate of retention of vocabulary items in the basic core is constant through time, that the rate of loss of basic vocabulary is approximately the same in all languages, and that, if the percentage of true cognates within the core vocabulary is known for any pair of languages, the length of time that has elapsed since the two languages began to diverge from a single language can be computed according to the following formula:

(8.1)

$$t = \frac{\log C}{2 \log r}$$

where t is the time depth in millennia, C is the percent of cognates, and r is the glottochronological constant, the percent of cognates assumed to remain after a thousand years of divergent development. For the 100-word list, the glottochronological constant is claimed to be 86 percent; for the 200-word list it is 81 percent.

Although some scholars have welcomed glottochronology as a method for establishing relationships between languages for which no written evidence exists, others have called even the basic assumptions into question. At least three problems have to be considered before glottochronology can be accepted as a valid technique in historical linguistics. First of all, is the list representative? Are the words contained in the list really the common core shared by all languages? Is it a fact that the items included in the list are not culture-bound? There exists no systematic study that would show that the words in the list are either less likely or more likely to be borrowed than words in some other list established according to a different set of criteria.

Better documented is the criticism directed at the claim that the retention rate is the same for all languages, and that the glottochronological constant has the values attributed to it by Swadesh. Bergsland and Vogt (1962) found 100 percent retention in Modern Icelandic, 43 percent for Eskimo, 96.7 percent for Armenian, and 96.5 percent for Georgian, for the 100-word list, whose standard rate is supposed to be 86 percent. Bergsland and Vogt explain the discrepancies through the conservative nature of traditional societies in the cases of Icelandic, Armenian and Georgian, and through the effect of word taboo in Eskimo, taboo there being a cultural phenomenon that leads to avoidance and rapid displacement of that part of the vocabulary that is associated with recently died persons. In presenting the counterexamples, Bergsland and Vogt certainly have made their point: retention rate is not constant. The rate of retention depends on both external and internal circumstances of the societies that use the language, and the results obtained by use of the constant can be just as far from the truth in the cases in which the method is applied to previously untested languages as they turned out to be in the test cases considered by Bergsland and Vogt.

Even more basic is the question about the validity of the hypothesis underlying all glottochronological work, the hypothesis that language change takes place according to the family tree hypothesis and that languages diverge from each other as a result of successive splits. Later contacts between languages can influence the calculations, and in many cases they obscure the true picture.

But even without complications introduced by borrowing, the situation is difficult enough. As far as the phonetic shape of words is concerned, there are two possibilities. Either true cognates may not be recognizable because of sound changes (compare the English word *tooth* with the German word *Zahn*), or chance similarities may be interpreted as evidence for the presence of a true cognate pair (the Latin verb *habere* and the German verb *haben* both mean 'to have', for example).

Overestimation of cognates results in underestimation of time depth and vice versa. As far as the meaning of words is concerned, true cognates may be rejected because in one or both languages a semantic change may have taken place. Furthermore, what should one do in cases where the original word, a true cognate, survives in the language side by side with a newly introduced word? For example, the Swadesh list contains the English word *grease*, for which the German equivalent is *Fett*. But *fat* survives in English, side by side with the Romance loanword *grease*—probably in its more basic meaning. The Swadesh list contains the English word *flesh*, translated into German as *Fleisch*. Here the identification of the two words as cognates suppresses an existing difference, since the meaning of German *Fleisch* is really better expressed with the English word *meat*, a Germanic word this time, whose scope of reference has undergone narrowing in English from 'food' to 'flesh of animals used for eating'. The English list contains the word *tree*, for which the German equivalent is *Baum*. Since *beam* exists in English too, are the sound changes and semantic changes that have taken place sufficient to make us reject *beam* as a cognate of German *Baum*? Decisions like these have to be made for practically every word on the glottochronological list, and the calculation of time depths depends crucially on the number of correctly identified cognates.

We have compared English and Latvian, finding eighteen cognates and calculating the time depth as 5,679 years. We also have calculated the effect of making a single mistake in identifying the cognates correctly. If we had discovered only seventeen cognates (assuming that we failed to identify a true cognate pair), the time depth would have been 5,868 years, with an overestimation of 189 years; had we found nineteen cognates (assuming that we had wrongly identified a pair of words as cognates when they were actually unrelated), the time depth would have been 5,500 years, with an underestimation of 179 years. The effect of making even a minimal change in the glottochronological constant would be even larger (and recall here the evidence presented by Bergsland

and Vogt to the effect that the precise claims are probably false). If the glottochronological constant were 85 percent instead of the postulated 86 percent, the time depth between the two languages would be 5,261 years, with a difference of 418 years. It is probably fair to say that the reliability of glottochronology as a method for establishing time depths remains to be established.

RECOMMENDED READING

Bergsland, K., and H. Vogt. (1962) "On the Validity of Glottochronology," *Current Anthropology* 3, 115-153.

Bloomfield, L. (1933) *Language*, Holt, Rinehart and Winston, New York, chapter 24.

Hymes, D. (1960) "Lexicostatistics So Far," *Current Anthropology* 1, 3-44.

Mallory, J. (1973) "A Short History of the Indo-European Problem," *Journal of Indo-European Studies* 1, 21-65.

Sturtevant, E. (1917) *Linguistic Change,* University of Chicago Press, Chicago, Illinois, chapters 4 and 5.

Swadesh, M. (1950) "Salish Internal Relationships," *IJAL*, 157-167.

Szemerenyi, O. (1962) Principles of Etymological Research in the Indo-European Languages. 2. Fachtagung für indogermanische und allgemeine Sprachwissenschaft. *Innsbrucker Beiträge zur Kulturwissenschaft* 15, 175-212.

CHAPTER NINE
LANGUAGE CONTACT AND
LINGUISTIC CHANGE

In chapter 2 we noted that comparative reconstruction is sometimes hindered by the presence of borrowed items in one or more of the languages under comparison. Except for that observation and references to the social motivation for language change, the discussion of diachronic processes has thus far been largely concerned with dynamic developments that are apparently motivated internally, that is, by changing structural relationships among the subsystems constituting individual languages. It is commonplace, however, for languages to undergo change as a result of contact with other languages. The general term for language change due to language contact is *borrowing*. Language change through borrowing may be of two types: either the adoption of linguistic features from outside the main tradition of a language or the adoption of a language by a population for whom it is a second language with consequent alterations in the structure of the borrowed language.

Since language contact takes place basically in the linguistic usage of an individual who is bilingual to a certain degree, let us examine first language contact as it affects an individual and then the results of contact between linguistic communities. The limits of bilingualism can be drawn at different levels; the extreme cases would be, on the one hand, a person who uses a single borrowed word in his otherwise monolingual speech, and on the other hand, a person who commands two (or more) languages in a way that is indistinguishable from the usage of a monolingual native speaker of each of the bilingual's languages. More practically, a bilingual speaker might be described as a person who can express himself in spontaneous, intelligible sentences in at least one language in addition to his first language.

EFFECTS OF PHONIC INTERFERENCE

A certain amount of interference exists between the two languages used by the bilingual speaker. Interference may occur at all linguistic levels—phonetic and phonological, morphosyntactic, and semantic. Interference arises when the bilingual speaker interprets linguistic features of his second language in terms of the linguistic features of his first language or, conversely, when he transfers elements from his second language into his first language.

Weinreich (1954) termed both phonetic and phonological interference *phonic interference*, and defined it as the manner in which a speaker perceives and reproduces the sounds of the secondary language in terms of the system of his primary language. There are four basic types of phonic interference:

1. *Underdifferentiation*. Two sounds are confused in the secondary system, if their counterparts are not distinguished in the primary system. For example, in Spanish, /d/ is a phoneme with two conditioned variants: [d] occurs in word-initial position and after [n], [ð] occurs in intervocalic position. The two sounds never contrast in identical environments. In English, /d/ and /ð/ are separate phonemes. A speaker of Spanish who is learning English is likely to treat the English /d/ and /ð/ as allophones of one phoneme, failing to note and produce the contrast in words like *day* and *they*.

2. *Overdifferentiation*. This term is used to refer to the imposition of phonemic distinctions from the primary system to the sounds of the secondary system, where they are not required. For example, speakers of Thai distinguish between /d/, /t/ and /t^h/ as separate phonemes. Learning English, they may identify the English unaspirated [t] in words like *stop* with their own /t/, and the aspirated [t^h] in words like *top* with their own /t^h/. Whereas underdifferentiation often contributes to a "foreign accent," overdifferentiation can seldom be perceived by the listener, provided the phonetic realizations of the phonemes of one language and allophones of the other language are sufficiently similar.

3. *Reinterpretation of distinctions*. This occurs when a bi-

lingual distinguishes phonemes in the secondary system by features merely concomitant or redundant in that system but relevant in his primary system. For example, a speaker of Finnish—a language with distinctive vowel length—may disregard the vowel quality difference in English words like *bit* and *beat* and distinguish between these and similar words on the basis of the difference in the duration of the two syllable nuclei.

4. *Phone substitution.* In this type of interference, phonemes are identically defined in two languages, but their normal pronunciation differs. Many foreign accents are primarily due to phone substitutions, such as the use of a tongue-tip trill for /r/ in English by native speakers of Spanish or Russian, a dental or retroflex /t/ by speakers of Hindi, or failure to velarize word-final /l/ by speakers of German.

MORPHOSYNTACTIC INTERFERENCE

Similar kinds of interference can be observed at the morphosyntactic level. If a distinction is lacking in the primary language, the bilingual speaker is likely to neutralize it in the secondary language. Hungarian, for example, lacks grammatical gender; gender is, however, an obligatory grammatical category in German. A speaker of Hungarian (or of English, for that matter) is likely to confuse genders in German. Chinese lacks an overt number category, which is obligatory in English. A speaker of Chinese frequently combines a plural subject with a singular verb and vice versa when speaking English.

On the other hand, if the primary language possesses a distinction that is lacking in a secondary language, the distinction is carried over into the secondary language. This would correspond *mutatis mutandis* to phonic overdifferentiation, just as the previously described kind of interference would correspond to phonic underdifferentiation. This becomes particularly apparent when a word from the secondary language is borrowed into the primary language. For example, Turkish possesses neither grammatical gender in substantives nor aspectual distinctions in verbs. When a fairly large number of Turkish loanwords entered Serbocroatian, they were assigned gender and aspect according to the system characteristic of Serbocroatian.

An example of reinterpretation of distinctions is provided by the following case. Let us assume that a bilingual's primary language uses fixed word order to signal relationships between words in a sentence (English with subject – verb – object order would be such a language). The secondary language possesses a rich inflectional system; relationships between words are signaled primarily by inflectional suffixes, but one of many possible word orders occurs more frequently than others (Latin would be a language of this type, with predominant subject – object – verb order). An English-speaking student of Latin is likely to interpret word order in Latin as distinctive, thus reinterpreting a redundant feature as a distinctive one.

Outright substitution of one construction for another is quite frequent in the speech of many bilinguals; so-called literal translations fall into this category, which is comparable to phone substitutions at the phonetic level. Some second-generation German Americans who speak quite fluent German replace colloquial standard German constructions like *Wie heisst du*? (lit.) 'How are you called?' with *Was ist dein Name*? (lit.) 'What is your name?' These literal translations frequently occupy the borderline between syntactic and lexical interference.

EFFECTS OF LANGUAGE CONTACT

Language contact is one of the main causes of lexical change in a language, involving semantic change in existing lexical items, addition of new words for new concepts, and replacement of native words by borrowed ones, and sometimes resulting in the restructuring of the whole vocabulary.

Before considering the effects language contact may have in bringing about language change, let us broaden the scope of our discussion from the bilingual individual to the linguistic community of which he is a part. When groups of speakers of two different languages come into contact, there are three possible outcomes depending on complex factors such as the military prowess of each group, their numbers, and their relative level of cultural development. In one situation, a group of invaders conquers the land of an indigenous population. After a longer or shorter period of bilingualism, the conquered people adopt the language of the conquerors. They carry over into their adopted language some features of their former primary language. The latter is said to constitute the *substratum* of the variety of the language of the conquerors ultimately spoken by descendants of the conquered population. Certain characteristics of English as it is spoken in Wales and Ireland are considered to be due to a Celtic substratum. Typically, though not exclusively, substratum effects are found in the phonology; in this sense the substratum is comparable to what seems to be the foreign accent of a bilingual in his secondary language.

If the number of invaders is small, and particularly if their cultural level is deemed inferior to that of the conquered indigenous population, the outcome may be quite different; the conquerors may adopt the language of the local population and be absorbed into it linguistically and culturally. Their language often survives in a number of loanwords adopted by the speakers of the primary language. In this case, the language of the conquerors is called a *superstratum*. A case in point would be the conquest of what is now France by a Germanic tribe, the Franks, who left little linguistically beyond a number of loanwords—characteristically connected with warfare—and their name, which was extended to both the territory and the originally Romance-language-speaking population.

The effects of a superstratum are comparable to the effects of a bilingual's secondary language on his primary language. Many bilinguals introduce words from the secondary language into the primary language, especially if the primary language lacks words for new concepts with which the bilingual person has become acquainted through his contacts with speakers of the secondary language. We will discuss in greater detail the effects of the wholesale adoption of the language of one speech community by another later in this chapter.

A third situation is found in cases in which several language communities exist side by side over a long period of time, none of them giving up its own language in favor of another, but each of them influencing the others in various ways. In a relationship such as this, one language constitutes an *adstratum* for another language. In special cases, the languages may undergo similar developments, converging toward a common model. Such languages are found to share typological features, regardless of whether they are related or not. The German term *Sprachbund* (linguistic alliance) is applied to languages found in geographical areas where typological homogeneity is replacing genetic heterogeneity. (See Jakobson 1931 and 1938.)

The process through which linguistic innovations spread through such a language convergence area is that postulated by the wave theory. An important modification of the wave theory was provided by Jakobson, who introduced the concept of *linguistic affinity*. According to Jakobson (1938), a language will accept foreign structural elements only when they correspond to its own tendencies of development.

For example, Yiddish has developed an aspectual system (perfective/imperfective) on the model of Slavic languages with which it was in contact for centuries (Weinreich, 1953, p. 41). However, Yiddish, like other Germanic languages, already possessed (for certain pairs of verbs) prefixation, a device for indicating perfective aspect, which was similar to the principal device for marking perfective aspect in Slavic languages. Taking German and Russian as examples, we may compare German *kennen* 'to know' and *erkennen* 'to recognize' with Russian *znat'* 'to know' and *poznat'* 'to get to know'. Yiddish developed its aspectual system at least partly because the tendency for differentiating between the perfective and the imperfective aspect was already present in the language before the extensive contact with Slavic. To give an example from phonology, English is generally assumed to have added /v/ to its phonemic system through contact with Norman French. However, English already had a voiced and voiceless correlation within its consonant system (that is, practically all consonants occurred in voiced and voiceless pairs such as /p/ and /b/). Also, [v] was already present in the language as a positionally determined allophone of /f/, occurring in voiced environments (such as intervocalic position). The introduction of Norman French loanwords like *veal* introduced /v/ into positions in which it did not previously occur in English and thus made possible minimal pairs like *feel* and *veal*, thereby turning /v/ into an independent phoneme. It is unlikely that /v/ could have been introduced into the language without certain predispositions that already existed in English.

Language contact may result not only in the introduction of a new feature, but in the persistence of a feature that disappears in related languages that are members of different linguistic alliances. For example, Russian, Belorussian, Ukrainian, and Polish have lost an earlier quantity opposition in vowels; Czech and Western Slovak have retained (and elaborated) this distinction. The cause of the maintenance of quantity oppositions in Czech and Western Slovak may very likely be the close proximity of the German and especially the Hungarian linguistic territories, both languages possessing a length opposition. Speakers of Eastern Slovak, on the other hand, had closer contacts with speakers of Ukrainian; Eastern Slovak has lost the quantity distinction, while Western Slovak has retained it.

Another example of a language convergence area is found in Northern Europe, where speakers of rather remotely related languages have either maintained or introduced a tonal opposition. This language area surrounds the Baltic Sea. Tonal oppositions are found in Danish, Swedish, Norwegian, Latvian, Lithuanian, and Slovincian (a dialect of North Kashubian, a Western Slavic language). One might compare Icelandic, a geographically far-removed sister language of Norwegian, which has not developed a tonal opposition, and note that the Swedish of Finland has lost such an opposition—most probably because of an adstratum relationship with Finnish, which does not possess lexical tone.

The classic example of the Sprachbund phenomenon is provided by the Balkan case. The eventful history of the Balkans has created a situation in which language, ethnicity, nationalism, politics, religion and economy all contribute toward an exceptional sociocultural variety, and within it toward some even more fascinating similarities. The languages include several Slavic languages and dialects (Bulgarian, Macedonian, part of Serbocroatian), Romance languages and dialects (several varieties of Rumanian and Italian), Greek, Albanian, Turkish, and Hungarian. Various linguistic innovations, called *Balkanisms* in this context, are shared by two or more of these languages and dialects. The most widely distributed among the Balkanisms are the following:

1. Decay of nominal (and pronominal) inflection. This process seems to have gone farthest in Bulgarian, where the case system is almost totally eliminated, but it is shared to a greater or lesser extent by Macedonian, southeastern dialects of Serbocroatian, Modern Greek, Albanian, and Rumanian.

2. Pleonastic use of pronouns. A Bulgarian example would be *Mene mi se struva* 'It seems to me' (literally 'To me to me it seems'), where the first person pronoun is used twice. Similar constructions abound in Modern Greek, Rumanian, Albanian, and in Serbocroatian dialects spoken in the vicinity of the Bulgarian linguistic territory.

3. Loss of the infinitive and replacement of an infinitive construction by a personal one. In Bulgarian, the request "Give me to drink" is expressed as *Daj mi do pija* 'Give me that I drink'. Modern Greek has *Dos mou na pio*, translated identically. The phenomenon is also found in Albanian, Rumanian, Macedonian, and in the eastern dialects of Serbocroatian.

4. Development of a postpositional article. Slavic languages normally lack articles, but Bulgarian and Macedonian have developed them. Bulgarian contrasts *prijatel* 'friend' with *prijatelŭt* 'the friend', *žena* 'woman' with *ženata* 'the woman'. Similar developments are found in Rumanian (*prieten, prietenul* 'friend', 'the friend'), and Albanian (*mik, miku* 'friend', 'the friend'). Note that the form of the postpositional article has not been borrowed; each language has used material avail-

able in that language for producing a structurally similar result. Modern Greek has an article, but it occurs before the noun and is not suffigated (it does not constitute a bound morpheme attached to the end); other Balkan languages do not share this development.

5. Loss of tonal and quantity oppositions. The Southern Slavic area extends from the northwest to the southeast. Both tonal and quantity oppositions are fully manifested in the northwest (in Slovene and in the western dialects of Serbocroatian); in the eastern dialects of Serbocroatian the oppositions gradually lose their significance, until in Macedonian and Bulgarian they have been completely eliminated.

A number of minor Balkanisms are shared by two or more languages or dialects in the Balkan Sprachbund area. It should be emphasized, however, that there is no single language in the Balkans, either at an earlier stage or in the present day, that would contain all the features called Balkanisms and that might be assumed to be their source. The various substratum and superstratum relationships have all been investigated, but the Balkan case has resisted explanation on this basis. A suggestion has recently been put forward by Civ'jan (1965) that the Balkanisms cannot be explained through developments that have taken place in the past but rather must be explained through development toward a common structure in the future. The grammatical structures of the Balkan languages seem to be converging toward increasing similarity. It is possible to set up a sentence model toward which the languages are evolving; the sentence model would consist of the same syntactic slots, which may be filled by lexical items drawn from any one of the languages constituting the Sprachbund. In this way the Balkans constitute a *language convergence* area par excellence.

STRUCTURAL CHANGES DUE TO BORROWING

Let us now consider in some detail the kinds of structural changes that might affect languages due to borrowing. In his important and well-known *Language*, Bloomfield categorized the borrowing of linguistic features from one speech community to another as *cultural borrowing, intimate borrowing*, and *dialect borrowing*. Cultural borrowing is the adoption from a different language of linguistic forms (usually words) referring to notions and things newly introduced to one cultural group (the speakers of the borrowing language) from another (the speakers of the donor language). Cultural borrowing is associated with cultural diffusion. Intimate borrowing refers to the transfer of linguistic features between two languages spoken in what is geographically and politically a single community. Dialect borrowing is the adoption of linguistic features associated with speakers of a different ''form'' of the language of the recipient. The motivation for dialect borrowing is usually social.

EFFECTS OF CULTURAL BORROWING

Cultural borrowing often operates in both directions between languages in cultural contact, and it affects the speech of individuals who are fundamentally monolingual. Currently, speakers of English and French are in cultural contact, and the words for borrowings from one culture are commonly introduced into the language of the recipient culture along with the novelty itself. In the United States we find restaurants where the basic form for all dishes is a very thin pancake, stuffed with a great variety of fillings. This borrowing from French cuisine is called in America a *crepe* (after French, *la crêpe*), and the restaurants where they are prepared are often termed *creperies* (after French *une crêperie*). Similarly, in Paris, one may order *le milk shake*, a drink originating in America and called by its American name in France.

Cultural borrowing is one-sided when the cultural diffusion with which it is associated is itself unidirectional. For example, when Christianity was introduced into England by continental missionaries in the seventh century, there came into English many Latin and Greek terms for institutions and apparatus associated with that religion; *minister, angel, devil, apostle, bishop, priest, monk, nun, mass, marble* are just a few.

It should be noted that borrowed words are, for the most

part, totally absorbed into the phonological and morphological systems of the borrowing language. In the initial stages, borrowed words are partly or fully integrated into the borrowing language. Unfamiliar sounds are replaced by the sounds that seem most similar to speakers of the borrowing language; syllable-structure and word-structure rules of the borrowing language are applied to the new words. The words are supplied with any lacking grammatical categories and integrated into the grammatical system. If, for example, a potential borrowing does not conform to the phonological system of the recipient language, an alteration in its phonetic shape will be part of the borrowing process. For example, the initial segment in French *crêpe* is not aspirated; it is [k]. However, English does not permit word-initial unaspirated voiceless stops. Hence English `crepe` is pronounced with initial [k^h].

Important for reconstructing the history of two languages whose speakers are in cultural contact is the fact that from the moment of borrowing, the loanword stops participating in the sound changes of its language of origin and begins to participate in the sound changes taking place in the language into which it was borrowed. In many instances, this makes it possible to establish the phonetic values of sounds whose spelling does not reflect the changes that have occurred in their realization. For example, when the Latin word *cellarium* `cellar` appears in German as a loanword in the form *Keller,* we may conclude that the sound spelled with *c* in Latin was still pronounced as a stop at the time of the borrowing. When the Latin word *cella* `cell` appears in German as *Zelle*, we may conclude that the Latin sound change, $k > ts$, took place between the dates at which the two words were borrowed into the ancestor language of present-day German.

If the number of loanwords is large and the contact lasts for a sufficient length of time, the borrowing language may undergo some structural changes. New sequence patterns may be created; allophones that were formerly positional variants may appear in positions from which they were formerly excluded, resulting in the development of new phonemic oppositions; the pronunciation of sounds may change, and new sounds may be introduced; formerly exceptionless patterns may become submerged in so numerous exceptions that the pattern loses its force and acquires the status of one of many idiosyncratic subpatterns. There are many instances of developments of this type.

During a relatively short but very significant period of contact between English and Scandinavian speakers in the northern part of Britain in the eleventh century, for example, many Scandinavian words were borrowed into English. As a result of a very early English sound change, the initial cluster [sk] becomes [š]; compare Old English *scōh* [skōx], *scip* [skip] with Modern English *shoe* [šu], *ship* [šɪp]. Scandinavian borrowings like *sky, skin, scatter,* and *skirt* (compare with native *shirt*) reintroduced the initial cluster [sk]. Changes in the grammatical systems of languages resulting from borrowing are far more likely in situations of intimate borrowing.

A particularly interesting type of cultural borrowing is the *loan translation*. In instances of loan translation, the model in the language of origin is translated, morpheme by morpheme, in the recipient language. A classic example is the French loan translation, *gratte-ciel* (literally '(that which) scrapes the sky') from English *skyscraper*. Similarly the Latin word *conscientia* (formed by combining the prefix *cum* 'with' and the noun *scientia* 'knowledge', which developed into French *conscience*, and was subsequently borrowed into English) is a loan translation from Ancient Greek *syneidēsis* (*syn* 'with' + *eidēsis* 'knowledge').

Loanwords are not all integrated to the same degree. There appears to be a continuum between complete assimilation and complete *code-switching*. Code-switching refers to a situation in which speakers shift from one language or language variety to another depending on the situation. In most cases it is possible to locate a word fairly precisely on that continuum. For example the French word *paletot* 'overcoat' was borrowed into Russian in the nineteenth century and has been completely integrated into the phonological structure of Russian (in the form [pal'tó]). However, it continues to be marked as a foreign element in the lexicon because it remains uninflected in all cases of the singular and plural. *Paletot* is masculine in French; in Russian it has been assigned to the neuter gender like native Russian nouns ending in -*o*. (Gender is an obligatory category in Russian; in the case of an uninflected word like [*pal'to*], its gender becomes apparent when the word is combined with an adjectival attribute.) Thus while the phonological integration is complete, the morphological integration has only just begun.

EFFECTS OF INTIMATE BORROWING

Intimate borrowing is commonly the result of some historical event such as conquest or annexation (the Norman conquest of England in the eleventh century) or of massive peaceful migration (the European immigration to America in the nineteenth century). Intimate borrowing, unlike cultural borrowing, is not limited to cultural novelties, and is commonly one-sided, proceeding from the language of the dominant group to the language of the group that has come under domination. In intimate borrowing situations it is generally the case that at least one of the two groups of speakers in contact approaches bilingualism, and the probability is high that a language shift will ultimately take place.

The nature of the social relationships that obtain between language groups in an intimate borrowing situation is generally apparent in the borrowings themselves. In the case of the borrowings from Norman French into English from the eleventh to the thirteenth centuries, it is apparent that the Normans controlled the state, the military, the church, the arts, and the like. The evidence is the sets of borrowed words in (9.1).

(9.1)

a. government: *state, crown, reign, power, country, people, prince, duke, count*

b. law: *judge, jury, just, sue, plea, cause, accuse, crime, marry*

c. warfare: *battle, arms, soldier, officer, navy, enemy, siege, danger*

d. religion and morals: *religion, virgin, saint, pray, virtue, mercy*

e. hunting and other sports: *leash, falcon, scent, track, cards, dice, ace, suit, trump*

f. culture and the arts: *honor, glory, fine, noble, art, beauty, color, figure, paint, tower, palace, castle.*

That the Anglo-Saxons performed household services for their Norman conquerors is also apparent from the widespread borrowing of terminology associated with household duties and servitude, like these:

(9.2)
chair, table, furniture, serve, soup, fruit, jelly, boil, fry, roast, toast.

It is especially noteworthy that as a result of the Anglo-Norman linguistic contact, Modern English exhibits the unusual lexical dichotomy of having one set of words for meat on the hoof—*cow/ox, calf, swine, sheep*—and another for meat (of the same animal) on the table—*beef, veal, pork, mutton.* The former set of words is Germanic and native to English, whereas the second is the result of borrowing from Norman French. The French words were obviously used by speakers of English when they served at French tables, while the Anglo-Saxon words came to be reserved for use on the farm.

With the massive borrowing of words that generally occurs in intimate borrowing situations, phonological change is commonplace. We have already noted that in Old English /f/ had voiceless allophones in word-initial and word-final position and voiced allophones in voiced environments, for example, in the intervocalic position. Norman French loanwords introduced /v/ in word-initial position (in words like *veal, voice, very*) and thus contributed toward establishing /v/ as a separate phoneme in English. Recall also the reintroduction of initial *sk* in English from Scandinavian loanwords. Phonological change due to contact is not restricted to intimate borrowing situations. Intensive or prolonged cultural contact might produce sufficient lexical borrowing for phonological innovations to occur. In Czech, for example, /g/ had become /h/ at a relatively early stage; loanwords with /g/ reintroduced the sound into the language and restored the /g/ versus /k/ opposition. In Finnish, long /ee/ had diphthongized to /ie/; loanwords produced minimal pairs like *tie* 'road' versus *tee* 'tea', presenting the speakers with the problem of having to know the history of the word before applying the diphthongization rule—or, more likely, forcing the child learning the language to restructure it in such a way that diphthongization ceases to be recoverable as a synchronic rule of Finnish.

The morphological system, too, may show significant innovations due to massive borrowing. Language contact may, for example, result in the introduction of new suffixes. There appears to be an intermediate stage where the suffix appears only together with borrowed stems, and one cannot tell whether the morphologically complex word was borrowed as a whole or was produced through the addition of a suffix within the borrowing language. If the new suffix appears in conjunction with native stems, the suffixation process has become productive and a new suffix has been added to the borrowing language. If English had only words like *legible, edible, palatable,* we could not be sure whether *-ible, -able* is a productive suffix; the full integration of the suffix into the structure of English is attested with the appearance of words like *readable* and *eatable, doable* and *get-at-able*.

It will have become apparent by now that the part of language that is most susceptible to change through contact is its lexicon. A language can absorb large numbers of loanwords and still remain structurally relatively intact. The immense numbers of Norman French loanwords in English have not altered its basically Germanic structure. Rumanian morphology is almost purely Romance, and the language is still considered to be a Romance language, even though words of Latin origin constitute a minority of its vocabulary. In a recent Dacorumanian word list of 5,765 items, only 1,165 words (or approximately 20 percent) were descendants of Latin words. The vocabulary of the analyzed dialect was predominantly Slavic; 2,361 words, or approximately 41 percent of the words, were of Slavic origin, the rest being Turkish, Hungarian, Modern Greek, and Thracian.

Loanwords are important indicators of cultural contact, and, as we have seen, they can be used to reconstruct certain aspects of the history of the peoples involved in the contact situation. Frequently, however, the native word continues to exist side by side with the borrowed word. The semantic scope of the older word may be narrowed, or the two words may acquire different stylistic values. The English word *tell* experienced a reduction in its former scope with the introduction of the loanword *count*; the original meaning survives in the (now idiomatic) usage *telling one's beads,* and in job titles like *bank teller. Read* continued side by side with the newly introduced *peruse*; the latter, however, carries with it a stylistic connotation of solemnity and pedantry. When a borrowed word has the same etymological source as a native word, the two items are termed *etymological doublets.* Recall, for example, that native English *shirt* and the borrowed Scandinavian *skirt* have the same Proto-Germanic source. Etymological doublets (or for that matter triplets and so on) may all come from outside the main tradition of the borrowing language. The English words *state* and *estate* were both borrowed from middle French in which they were variants, and *status* is a relatively modern borrowing of the Latin word *status*, from which both *state* and *estate* are derived.

EFFECTS OF DIALECT BORROWING

The case of dialect borrowing is somewhat different from the kinds of developments that we have considered thus far in this chapter. Dialect borrowing often affects the very core of the speech of a linguistic community. Through dialect borrowing, changes affecting the basic structural system of the language of some group often occur. It should not be surprising that closely related dialects might influence one another more readily and more significantly than do foreign languages, since the similarities between the grammatical and lexical systems of two (or more) such groups will permit differences to be more easily interpreted. Labov and others have attempted to demonstrate that almost all changes might be accounted for through dialect borrowing.

In cultural and intimate contact situations, the major vehicle of cross-linguistic innovation was the word. When one dialect of a language exerts influence on another, various linguistic features, such as the pronunciation of a phoneme, a morphological or syntactic pattern, or the meaning of a word, may be borrowed. The spread of linguistic features from one dialect to another may proceed across geographic or social boundaries. When the domain of dialect borrowing is a geographic region, it is usually the case that the spread occurs within an area inhabited by peoples who are culturally and linguistically related. One town or province may develop as a political or cultural center and, hence, serve as a linguistic center from which innovations spread. The line that might be drawn on a map to surround the geographic area within which some linguistic feature or innovation has spread is termed an *isogloss*. The spread of innovations through social classes has been studied by sociolinguists.

As mentioned earlier, the wholesale adoption of a new language by a linguistic community represents an important context in which language change through contact might occur. In such situations it is usually the substratum language that effects significant changes on the successor language. This results from the fact that speakers interpret the patterns of a new language in terms of patterns already familiar to them from their own language. This is true in instances of lexical borrowing, and we perceive it whenever we hear someone speak with a foreign accent.

A particularly telling example of this sort of development can be seen in the English of Ireland, Hiberno-English (HE). English was for many years the socially and politically dominant language of Ireland where the native language was, and in some regions remains, Irish (Gaelic). The vast majority of features characterizing the particular form of English spoken in Ireland result from Irish substratum influence. For example, on the phonological level, some dialects of HE replace the Standard English correlation t/d : $\theta/\eth$ with a dichotomy between so-called broad and slender dental consonants respectively. For present purposes we may say that slender consonants are more palatal. Irish has no interdental fricatives, but it makes a phonemic distinction between broad and slender consonants. Irish is the obvious source of this HE innovation. An English opposition has been reinterpreted in terms of an Irish one.

Similarly on the syntactic level, it is a characteristic feature of HE that in almost every sentence some word is *topicalized*, or brought forward, resulting in a complex sentence with a relative clause. In colloquial HE one would rarely hear the sentence *I'm going to Dublin tomorrow*. Rather, one of the following would be preferred:

(9.3)
a. It's me that's going to Dublin tomorrow.
b. It's going that I am to Dublin tomorrow.
c. It's to Dublin that I'm going tomorrow.
d. It's Dublin that I'm going to tomorrow.
e. It's tomorrow that I'm going to Dublin.

Such patterns are the norm in all Celtic languages, and this particular feature of HE syntax, along with many more, is surely to be explained in terms of the Irish substratum. The English of Ireland has become, to a great extent, a series of literal translations of Irish.

RECONSTRUCTING A SUBSTRATUM

Even though the results of known language contacts can be described and the observed changes explained by assuming a causal relationship between the contact situation and the observed phenomena, it is by no means certain to what extent the processes can be reconstructed if and when the original characteristics of the languages involved are not known. To conclude this section, we would like to summarize briefly the results of an attempt to reconstruct a substratum solely from its effects on the bilingual speaker's second language (Lehiste 1965).

The attempt involved analysis of a lengthy poem written in Halbdeutsch—a kind of Baltic German based on an Estonian substratum. The language called Halbdeutsch was spoken by lower middle classes in small towns in Estonia in the nineteenth century. Changes in the social and political life of Estonia in the twentieth century have resulted in the disappearance of Halbdeutsch. During the nineteenth century it could have been speculated, however, that Halbdeutsch might become the prevailing language, and Estonian might disappear.

The author asked the hypothetical question: assuming that Estonian had disappeared, how much could we find out about it by analyzing Halbdeutsch? Since there is independent evidence for both Estonian and Baltic German, the analysis might make it possible to test our methodology and draw some inferences about the general problems connected with the reconstruction of a substratum.

The vowel system of Baltic German consists of eight short vowels—/i e ü ö u o a ə/, the /ə/ being restricted to unstressed syllables. It has eight long vowels—ī ē ɛ̄ ṻ ȫ ū ō ā, /ē/ and /ɛ̄/ contrasting in such words as *Beeren* 'berries' and *Bären* 'bears'. Estonian has nine vowels, which may occur in short, long, and overlong quantity—/i e ä u o a ö ü õ/, the last being a midcentral unrounded vowel. It has twenty-three diphthongs, most of which contrast long quantity with overlong quantity. Baltic German has six diphthongs. On the basis of the Halbdeutsch text, the Estonian vowel /õ/ could not be reconstructed, nor could the phonemic status of the opposition between /e/ and /ä/. Of the twenty-three Estonian and six Baltic German diphthongs, only two, /ei/ and /au/, appear in the Halbdeutsch. There would be no way even to guess at the extreme richness of the Estonian diphthongal inventory. The text also provides no basis for reconstructing the Estonian vowel quantity system.

In the consonant system, the main difference between Estonian and Baltic German is the absence of the voiced versus voiceless correlation in Estonian, the existence of a series of palatalized dentals in Estonian, where /t n l s/ contrast with /t' n' l' s'/, the presence of only one kind of sibilant in Estonian, and the existence of a three-way quantity opposition in Estonian consonants. The Halbdeutsch materials make it possible to reconstruct the absence of the voiced versus voiceless opposition in word-initial position. Furthermore, the numerical preponderance of /v/-substitutions for /f/ and /p t k/-substitutions for /b d g/ make it possible to assume the presence of /v/ and /p t k/ (and absence of /f/ and /b d g/) in the substratum language. It is also possible to reconstruct the existence of only one sibilant as well as its phonetic quality—/s/

—and the loss of word-initial /h/. The apparent simplification of initial clusters enables us to reconstruct a feature of the canonical shape of Estonian morphemes: lack of initial clusters. What cannot be reconstructed is the presence of a palatalized dental series, and the three-way quantity contrasts.

As regards morphology and syntax, it would be possible to reconstruct the absence of grammatical gender and absence of articles in the substratum. In the verbal system, one would notice a tendency to generalize the so-called weak conjugation, that is, to inflect strong verbs without change in the root vowel. One might conjecture that the substratum language had only regular verbs. This would be a gross oversimplification; the Estonian verbal system (as well as the nominal one) is characterized by complicated morphophonemic changes in the stem, even though ablaut of the Germanic kind is not present in Estonian.

The future in Halbdeutsch is formed with the auxiliary *wollen* instead of *werden*. To conclude that Estonian uses the equivalent of *wollen* as a future auxiliary would be totally misleading; Estonian has no future auxiliary and indeed provides no morphological device for indicating the future, except for the use of temporal adverbs signifying future time.

But the greatest opportunity for drawing wrong conclusions appears in the nominal inflection system. Baltic German has four cases; Estonian has fourteen. Both languages also mark the plural, so that Baltic German has eight case forms, Estonian has twenty-eight. Only one form appears in the Halbdeutsch text. The practically complete absence of noun inflection would make it impossible even to suspect the existence of the fourteen cases of Estonian with their twenty-eight different forms.

Thus the influence of the substratum upon the successor language consists mainly in eliminating or reducing contrasts rather than introducing new contrasts. (As we noted in the case of Hiberno-English, a reinterpretation of contrasts is also quite feasible.) It was possible to reconstruct the absence of a feature in the substratum on the basis of underdifferentiation in the successor language, provided we knew about that absence; but there is no way to distinguish these cases from the elimination of a contrast in the successor language in instances where the substratum language actually had greater complexity than the adopted language. It seems plausible enough to conclude that the absence of an opposition of voiced and voiceless in Estonian caused the loss of the distinction between voiced and voiceless in Halbdeutsch. Observing the absence of nominal inflection in Halbdeutsch as compared to Baltic German, one might analogously attribute the loss of case inflection to a presumed absence of case inflection in Estonian. This would be highly erroneous since Estonian actually had a very rich and complex case system. Thus the apparent loss of a contrast in a successor language does not always justify one to assume the absence of such contrasts in the substratum.

Several of the linguistic features of Halbdeutsch are reminiscent of *pidgins*, abbreviated forms of language arising from a need for communication among speakers of mutually unintelligible languages. When such a language is learned as a primary language, it is called a *creole,* a language in which some features of the original pidgin are developed further, while others are stabilized. The development of a new creole is an extraordinary diachronic development and is perhaps the most extreme result of language change due to language contact.

Unlike all other diachronic developments we have considered, creolization is not an example of the development of a language from one structural state to another. It represents the birth of a new language without the types of genetic ties we assume for most of the world's languages. The effects of pidginization and creolization on language history may well be grossly underestimated. See Hymes (1971) for a more complete discussion of this sociolinguistic phenomenon, the understanding of which may offer significant insights for diachronic studies.

RECOMMENDED READINGS

Bloomfield, L. (1933) *Language,* Holt, Rinehart and Winston, New York, chapters 25, 26, and 27.

Clyne, M. (1975) *Forschungsbericht Sprachkontakt,* Kronberg/Ts, Scriptor-Verlag.

Clyne, M. (1972) *Perspectives on Language Contact,* The Hawthorn Press, Melbourne.

Hall, R. A. (1965) *Pidgin and Creole Languages.* Cornell University Press, Ithaca, New York.

Haugen, E. (1959) *The Norwegian Language in America: A Study in Bilingual Behavior.* 2nd ed., Indiana University Press, Bloomington, Indiana.

Hymes, D., ed. (1971) *Pidginization and Creolization of Languages,* The University Press, Cambridge, England.

Jakobson, R. (1931) "Über die phonologischen Sprachbünde," *Travaux du Cercle Linguistique de Prague* 4, 234–240.

Jakobson, R. (1936) "Sur la theorie des affinités phonologiques entre les langues," in *Proceedings of the 4th International Congress of Linguists,* Copenhagen, pp. 277–287.

Lehiste, I. (1965) "A Poem in *Halbdeutsch* and Some Questions Concerning Substratum," *Word* 21, 55–69.

Sapir, E. (1921) *Language,* Harcourt, Brace and World, New York, chapter 9.

Weinreich, U. (1954) *Languages in Contact.* Linguistic Circle of New York, New York.

CHAPTER TEN
THE EVIDENCE

Although the development of sophisticated techniques for reconstruction permits a considerable expansion of the time depth within which language change can be investigated, it must be admitted that reconstructed languages are hypothetical and undocumented. The inevitable consequence is a substantial margin for error in theories about diachronic processes based on reconstructed languages. The existence of written records, however, especially in cultures with a long and unbroken tradition of writing, presents the historical linguist at once with a treasure chest of historical data upon which to base claims about language change, and with an empirical testing ground for theories of change based on synchronic models of grammar. A brief sketch of the development of writing offers some idea of the linguistic character of written records of ancient languages, which hold so much important information for the student of language change.

THE DEVELOPMENT OF WRITING

The precursor to writing is surely the drawings primitive peoples place on the walls of caves and other places of habitation in order to characterize important events. The earliest drawings have been discovered in caves in Spain, and date from approximately 15,000 B.C. Ultimately, representational drawings were replaced with *mnemonic devices,* or pictures reminding the viewer of a particular individual, thing, or occurrence, especially the name of a marked object's owner. From the point when the pictures come to refer consistently to a named object, individual, or event—when a given picture stands for a given word—we speak of a writing system. *Writing* is a system of picturelike symbols, finite in number and often highly stylized in form, which represent linguistic constituents. Such symbols may stand for words, morphemes, syllables, or sounds, but there is usually a regular (often one-to-one) correspondence between symbol and that which is symbolized.

The first writing systems were highly pictorial and transparent. A symbol like �⌡ in Sumerian represented the
word 'sun'. After the symbols became more stylized and
opaque with respect to their lexical referent they came to refer
to broadly defined notions; such symbols are called *ideographs*. Ultimately these same symbols develop a specific
lexical referent and are called *logographs*.

Of course a writing system with one symbol for every word
would quickly become very cumbersome and difficult to learn.
In the Chinese writing system, which remains largely ideographic, a system of radicals or root symbols is used in com-
bination with other symbols to make up words in order to limit
absolute diversity in the written representation of words. In
the writing systems of ancient Mesopotamia, which represent
the oldest known form of writing, one symbol often stood for
several different but related words. For example, in Sumerian,
the oldest attested language (about 3,000 B.C.), the same symbol, ⊷⊣ , is used for the words for 'god', *dingir* and 'heaven',
an.

The most important event in the simplification and sophis-
tication of writing was the transition from the purely ideographic or logographic to *phonographic* systems. A phonographic writing system makes use of symbols to represent
sounds or sequences of sounds without regard to meaning.
Thus, the Sumerian symbol ⊷⊣ came to stand not only
for notions like 'god' and 'heaven' but for the phonetic sequence -*an*- in any word. Likewise the Sum. symbol ⬚
for *šu* 'hand' was used for the word for 'hand' and the syllable
-*šu*-. A writing system in which the symbols represent syllables
is called a *syllabary*. The Sumerian writing system and those
of many of the other languages of the ancient world, such as
Akkadian and Hittite, which were based on the Sumerian
system, and Ancient Egyptian, which has a separate origin
but a quite similar history, are composite logosyllabic systems.

The final stage in the development of writing is the transition
from syllabaries to *alphabets*. An alphabet is ideally a writing
system in which each symbol represents a distinctive sound
of the language. Alphabets developed initially in Ancient

Greece in the ninth century B.C. from the borrowed syllabic writing systems used for Semitic languages. Because vowels are to a great extent predictable from context in Semitic languages, syllabic symbols came to be associated with consonants alone, rather than with consonant – vowel – consonant (CVC) sequences. When the system was revised to be useful for European languages, specific vowel symbols were developed, resulting in an alphabet.

The very character of the development of writing systems in the ancient world has posed problems for investigators attempting to read and analyze texts written in these early systems. Even if the language of a text is known, difficulties arise in determining which of many meanings associated with some ideographic symbol is to be understood, whether a given symbol is being used ideographically or phonographically, and many other issues. We can be fairly confident that every scribal tradition made use of conventions with respect to the use of a system of writing symbols. However, such conventions are themselves rarely written down or codified, and they must be inferred by modern students of ancient texts. The analysis, interpretation, and restoration of archaic texts is termed *philology*. Solid philological investigation is the foundation of most historical linguistic research. An even more basic endeavor relating to the linguistic analysis of texts is the decipherment of extinct writing systems.

DECIPHERING EXTINCT WRITING SYSTEMS

The most notable advances in the decipherment of ancient texts took place in the nineteenth century. The mysterious Egyptian *hieroglyphic* inscriptions and the *cuneiform* inscriptions both on monuments and clay tablets of the ancient Near East and Middle East captured the imagination of traditional scholars as well as amateur decipherers. The world *hieroglyphic* means sacred carving in Greek, and was used to describe ancient Egyptian writing. It has come to refer to any writing system consisting of picturelike symbols, where the picture-symbols may not reflect in any direct and obvious fashion the thing to which they refer. The word *cuneiform* means having the shape of a wedge (from Latin *cuneis* 'wedge') and refers to the wedge-shaped symbols of the logosyllabic writing systems of ancient Assyria, Persia, and Anatolia. The wedge-shaped symbols were generally made with a stylus in wet clay tablets.

The decipherment of ancient writing systems was aided significantly by the existence of bilingual and trilingual texts. The famous Rosetta Stone, discovered in the Nile Delta in 1899, is a trilingual text with three versions of one text, one in Ancient Egyptian hieroglyphics, a second in Neo-Egyptian in a more simplified writing system, and a third in Ancient Greek. Since Greek was a well-understood language at the time of the discovery of the Rosetta Stone, the meaning of the text was immediately clear. The task was to determine the structure of the Egyptian version.

The decipherment was aided significantly by the occurrence in the text of so-called *cartouches,* oblong figures that enclose the hieroglyphic characters constituting royal or divine names. Since the names were clear from the Greek version on the Rosetta Stone, phonetic values could be assigned to the Egyptian symbols on the basis of the pronunciation of names such as *Cleopatra* and *Ptolemy* marked by cartouches in the hieroglyphic text.

In the case of the decipherment of cuneiform writing, the problems were somewhat more difficult. Although bilingual and even trilingual texts were found, the languages of the texts were all written in cuneiform script. The first cuneiform language to be deciphered was Old Persian. Even though most of the inscriptions on monuments were trilingual (the other two languages of most inscription being Akkadian and Elamite), none of the languages was known, because the puzzle of the script had not been solved. Indeed, it was not even known what kind of writing system it was, whether it was an alphabet, syllabary, logosyllabary, or some other form. In 1802 Friedrich Münter noticed regular patterns in the inscriptions and made the brilliant guess that the patterns corresponded to the formulaic epithets of Persian royal personages, which were well known in later periods. The formula was of the form '*X, king, great king, king of kings, son of Y, . . .* ' where *X* and *Y* are the names of royal personages. Using information about the Old Persian line of succession and the Pehlevi (Middle Persian) pronunciation of the formula, phonetic values were suggested for individual cuneiform symbols. The hypothesis was correct and the pieces of the syllabary quickly fell into place. Once Old Persian was deciphered, it became possible to unravel the mysteries of Akkadian and Elamite, because many trilingual inscriptions existed. Moreover, because several Akkadian-Sumerian bilingual texts were available, the interpretation of Akkadian quickly led to the decipherment of the oldest recorded language, Sumerian.

It should be pointed out that there are many written documents whose language is as yet undeciphered. For example, the Mayan hieroglyphs of Mexico are only poorly understood, and the so-called Linear A texts of ancient Crete continue to defy analysis. As yet undiscovered archives may offer many new insights into the past as well as many new puzzles.

Even after decipherment, gaps in our knowledge of the structure of the deciphered language generally remain. These gaps are sometimes a result of the nature of the writing system, but more often reflect the nature of the texts themselves and the scope of their content. Because the Hittite writing system is partly logographic and partly phonographic we do not, for example, know the Hittite word for 'son', although 'son' is commonly represented symbolically in the many Hittite texts detailing issues of royal succession. The gap results from the fact that Hittite, despite the largely phonographic character of its writing system, conventionally uses the Sumerian logograph for the word 'son'. For many words, a logograph is sometimes used, but in other cases the word is spelled out in syllabic symbols. Since there occurs no instance of a phonographic representation of the very common word 'son', there remains a gap in our knowledge about the Hittite lexicon.

Old Persian offers a different, but very common type of problem, being written in syllabic cuneiform. The symbols used for Old Persian were not developed for that language; as a result of centuries of borrowings, they are ultimately derived from the phonographic versions of the Sumerian cuneiform symbols. The consequence is the use of a syllabary in Old Persian that is inappropriate to its phonology. Several problems of the following type result. The sound sequences *ti* and *tai* are both common in the language. However, the syllabary does not include a symbol for the syllable *ti*. When a symbol does not exist for a consonant plus vowel sequence, the convention in Old Persian writing is to use two symbols—the symbol for the relevant consonant plus *a*, followed by the symbol for the vowel. Hence, *ti* is spelled *ta-i*. *ta-i* is, however, also a possible characterization of *tai*.

It is probable that this ambiguity offered no difficulty for native speakers of Old Persian. Because they knew the vocabulary and rules of grammar of the language, disambiguation would be straightforward. Native speaker insight is not available to the scholar of ancient texts, and some of these ambiguities must be tolerated in a retrospective analysis of the texts of an extinct language.

The gaps of information that result from inefficient writing systems are not restricted to the composition of lexicon and the phonological shape of its members. Points of grammar are also sometimes obscured. As it happens, *ti* and *tai* are the forms of two different but related morphemes in Old Persian: *ti* is the verbal inflection for the third person singular present active, *tai* marks third person singular present medio-passive. Because these two endings can be written in the same way it is often impossible to determine whether a given Old Persian verb is in the active or medio-passive voice.

PHILOLOGY

We have already noted that the narrow scope of the content of ancient texts is itself a detriment to a full recovery of the grammar and vocabulary of the languages of inherited texts. Many extinct languages are known to us only through the medium of inscriptions on monuments. Old Persian is such a language, and virtually all monumental texts from that language detail the exploits, in particular the conquests, of the kings of ancient Persia. The nature of the texts obviously limits the quantity of information available to us about the language. Besides monumental texts, the majority of written specimens in the ancient world were religious or ritual texts, business records, and legal or other governmental documents. In some cases, as in situations where only business records have been recovered, we do not even have examples of complete sentences, and hence we may have little or no knowledge of the syntax of an attested language. Our acquaintance with certain languages is restricted to place and/or personal names. The study of names is called *onomastics*.

When texts are available and the language of the texts is understood, it is the philologist who attempts to determine the quality of those texts. The analysis of the philologist establishes how faithful a given text is in its representation of language. A great variety of factors conspire to contaminate the textual witnesses that serve as our only sources of information about languages no longer spoken. The most common factor in the contamination of texts is *scribal error*. It is always necessary to take into consideration the fact that any text discovered at an ancient site might represent a copy of a centuries-old original or for that matter, a copy of a copy many times removed from the source.

Clay tables, papyrus, parchment, and other media for writing used before the development of the printing press are quite fragile. Consequently, the tradition of making many copies of a text was established early, as was the policy of recopying texts to maintain important documents and records over time. The scribe entrusted with the copying of an important document may have spoken a dialect different from that of the original or a variety of the language centuries younger than that of the original. The text may easily have come to be contaminated inadvertently by forms, and in some cases constructions, more natural to the scribe than those actually occurring in the text being copied. The philologist seeks to isolate features of a text that are dialectally or chronologically inappropriate, and where possible the attempt is made to restore

altered texts with the aid of *parallel texts* or texts with passages closely parallel to those under scrutiny. Parallel texts or
passages are two or more examples of the same document or
piece of a document.

Another situation resulting in documents wherein the language is not a genuine reflection of the language purportedly
represented arises when the texts are translations. The earliest
written documents in Gothic, the oldest attested Germanic
language, and Old Church Slavic, the oldest attested Slavic
language, are translations from Greek. Although there is no
reason to believe that the phonology and morphology of these
two languages suffer any significant influence from Greek, the
sentence structure of Gothic and Old Church Slavic in the
biblical texts appears to many to contain imitations of Greek
syntactic patterns. The recognition of this kind of external
influence in an archaic text is extremely useful in evaluating
the relevance of the language of such texts in drawing inferences for diachronic theory. Obviously, proper philological
analysis of the texts of languages no longer spoken is crucial
to the success of attempts to make linguistic inferences on the
basis of descriptions of the languages of those texts and on
the basis of alleged historical developments induced from data
drawn from such texts.

In many instances, oral tradition provides valuable information about earlier stages of a language. As an example, let
us consider the kind of evidence provided by orally transmitted poetry. The earliest forms of North Germanic are found
in Runic inscriptions. However, early inscriptions are few in
number, and later inscriptions are written in a greatly simplified Runic alphabet (the younger futhark) that makes sound
changes difficult to document. The culture apparently did not
place a premium on writing, but it did accord considerable
respect to oral poetry, and the tenth and eleventh centuries
witnessed a flourishing of scaldic poetry composed in intricate
meters and employing highly elaborate formal poetic devices.
It often happens that scaldic poems preserve older Old Norse
forms than were current at the time when the poems were

written down. The poems of Egill Skallagrimsson may serve
as a concrete example.

Egill lived from about 901 to 982A.D. His poems were evi-
dently transmitted orally until his saga was written down (the
extant manuscripts date from the middle of the fourteenth
century). One of the most accomplished poets of his time,
Egill would not have permitted himself an impure rhyme; yet
in one of his poems, composed in 936, we find *a* rhyming with
ǫ (the result of *u*-umlaut of *a*). One is entitled to conclude that
at the time of the composition of the poem the phonetic difference between an unmodified *a* and an *a* modified by a
following -*u* was not as great as it had become by the time the
manuscript was written, for by the later time different letters
are used for the two sounds. In another of his poems, composed in 962, Egill uses a meter that alternates lines of three
and four syllables. Because of his use of the word *braa* 'eye-
brows' (gen. pl.) in a metric foot where two syllables are
expected, we may conclude that the contraction of *braa* into
monosyllabic *brá* had not yet taken place.

Similar kinds of evidence can be found in folk songs. For
example, Finnish and Estonian folk songs are written in a
meter in which the basic unit is an eight-syllable line. The folk
song meter dates from a time at which Estonian had not yet
undergone various phonological processes that have resulted
in the loss of one or more syllables in a large number of words.
The requirement that a folk song line must contain eight syllables has preserved many earlier forms that have long since
disappeared from the spoken language.

The linguistic record we inherit through oral tradition offers
the historical linguist a significantly greater quantity and variety of data upon which to base diachronic descriptions and
theories, but the nature of the material and that same variety
often present complications of a type less prevalent in the
written record. Much of the traditional oral literature maintained by cultures over centuries represents codifications of
shorter formulaic texts, which were recited or chanted in different forms at a variety of places and times. The language of
the epic poems of Ancient Greece (1000–800 B.C.), for exam-

ple, does not represent the kind of coherent and consistent linguistic system generally used by the speakers of a particular speech community at a given point in time. Although the authorship of the Iliad and the Odyssey is traditionally attributed to a single individual, Homer, these poems include forms and constructions drawn from a variety of dialects to be distinguished both regionally and diachronically.

The stories constituting the Homeric poems were surely sung by bards all over Ancient Greece for many centuries before particular versions of each story came to be collected from various sources into the two composite works we refer to as the Iliad and the Odyssey. Just as these two great poems are literary composites, they are also linguistic composites. The pieces making up the whole are themselves versions of shorter stories, each codified in a particular region at a particular time. The result is a text that might be said to offer a *mixed language*, as all of the forms and constructions occurring in the poems were once extant among some group of Ancient Greek speakers, but we can be quite confident that no one ever spoke a dialect incorporating all of the linguistic constructs we confront in them. It is the task of the philologist to analyze texts such as the Homeric poems in order to clarify the dialectal and chronological facts. In the case of Ancient Greek, the scholar is aided greatly by the availability of later inscriptional and literary records for many of the dialects descended from those represented in the Iliad and the Odyssey.

The case of the Indo-European language of Ancient India offers a similarly complex situation. Although we inherit an enormous quantity of external material in Ancient Indic languages, that inheritance is entirely the consequence of a highly developed system of oral transmission. The earliest writing of which we have concrete evidence in India dates from the second century B.C. The Buddhist emperor Aśoka commissioned rules of conduct to be inscribed on pillars at several places in north India in the vernacular of the region. The language of those inscriptions is termed Middle Indic, a language significantly more recent than the language of oral tradition which dates to a period no later than 1000 B.C.

Our oldest Indian text is the Rig Veda, which was first written down and published in the nineteenth century after its discovery by Europeans. The text comprises ten books of hymns glorifying Hindu gods. It had been transmitted through the centuries in schools of priests (Brahmins), having been recited by rote in sacred contexts by chanters who often did not know the meaning of the ancient verses they had memorized. As in the case of the Homeric poetry, the Vedic language is a composite. Sets of hymns were developed by several Brahmin families. Consequently individual groups of hymns have their sources in different regions of north India and show considerable variety with respect to linguistic antiquity. The Rig Veda is assumed to have been codified in approximately 1000 B.C. and is organized according to principles other than linguistic ones. Some individual hymns consist of verses which are from different periods or dialectally distinct. Although scholars are in agreement with respect to many aspects of the dating of the Rig Veda, there remain many matters of controversy, and the philological analysis of the text remains an important research concern.

In the case of mixed-language texts, like the Homeric poetry and the Vedic hymns, hypotheses about the relative antiquity of forms and constructions are of crucial interest to the historical linguist. An incorrect analysis can result in ill-conceived reconstructions or mistaken histories. In either event, any theory about linguistic change that might depend on the validity of such reconstructions or proposed diachronic processes is likely to prove wrong. As always, when dealing with languages that are no longer extant, a thorough and informed philological analysis is crucially important to the linguistic investigation.

RECOMMENDED READINGS

Bloomfield, L. (1933) *Language*, Holt, Rinehart and Winston, New York, chapter 17.

Cleator, P. E. (1959) *Lost Languages*, Mentor Books, New York.

Friedrich, J. (1957) *Extinct Languages,* The Philosophical Library, New York.

Gelb, I. J. (1963) *A Study of Writing,* 2nd ed., University of Chicago Press, Chicago, Illinois.

Parry, M. (1971) *The Making of Homeric Verse,* Clarendon Press, Oxford.

GLOSSARY

ablaut
Morphologically conditioned alternations of vowels within a paradigm.

absolute merger
Total loss of a phonological distinction. Compare **absolute neutralization.**

absolute neutralization
Total loss of a phonetic difference between two or more phonologically distinct segments. Compare **absolute merger.**

actuation of sound change
Initiation of the event of change.

adjacent assimilation
Assimilation conditioned by an immediately preceding or following sound.

adstratum
One of two (or more) languages spoken within an area by people who maintain their primary languages while receiving influences from the other languages involved in the contact situation.

analogic creation
Introduction of new patterns into a language on the basis of preexisting structural patterns.

analogic extension
Replacement of old patterns in a language on the basis of preexisting structural patterns.

analogic restoration
Restoration of older forms (which had undergone phonetic change) through processes of **analogy.**

analogy
A linguistic process involving generalization of a relationship from one set of conditions to another set of conditions.

anaptyxis
Development of an epenthetic vowel that agrees in some feature with an adjacent sound.

anticipatory assimilation
See **regressive assimilation.**

aphaeresis
See **aphesis.**

aphesis
Loss of an initial vowel.

apocope
Loss of a final vowel.

assimilation
Process whereby two sounds in sequence become more similar to each other.

back formation
An analogic process involving reinterpretation of the morphological structure of a word.

Balkanisms
Linguistic innovations shared by languages that are members of the Balkan **Sprachbund.**

bleeding order
Application of two rules, A and B, so that the operation of A alters forms to which B might otherwise apply.

blend
A new word resulting from the contraction of two existing words.

borrowing
Language change due to language contact.

coalescence
See **merger.**

code switching
A situation in which speakers shift from one language or language variety to another depending on the situation.

coéfficients sonantiques
Segments reconstructed by Ferdinand de Saussure to account for the presence and quality of long vowels that occur in some Indo-European roots in the normal grade. Now called **laryngeals.**

cognates
Words that have descended from one and the same word of the protolanguage.

coinage
Creation of new words.

common innovations
See **shared innovations.**

common language
That stage in the historical development of a language that immediately precedes dialectal differentiation.

comparative reconstruction
Procedure for reconstructing a **protolanguage** by comparing **cognate** words in **daughter languages.**

compensatory lengthening
Lengthening of a sound associated with the loss of a subsequent sound.

complete merger
See **absolute neutralization.**

conditioned sound change
Sound change that affects sounds in certain identifiable phonetic environments.

contamination
Leveling within a semantic paradigm, that is, leveling within a set of words or morphemes that belong to a class that is defined by some close semantic relationship.

context-free sound change
See **unconditioned sound change.**

context-sensitive sound change
See **conditioned sound change.**

correspondences
See **sound correspondences.**

counter-bleeding order
Application of two rules, A and B, so that the operation of A alters

forms to which B might otherwise apply, but the reverse order (B preceding A) does not result in B feeding A. Compare **feeding order.**

counter-feeding order
Application of two rules, A and B, so that the output of A produces a form to which B will apply, but the reverse order (B preceding A) does not result in B bleeding A. Compare **bleeding order.**

creole
A pidgin learned as a primary language, in which some features of the original pidgin are developed further, while others are stabilized.

cultural borrowing
Adoption of linguistic forms (usually words) referring to notions and objects newly introduced to one cultural group from the language of the cultural group providing the new objects.

cuneiform
Term referring to wedge-shaped symbols, generally made with a stylus in wet clay tablets, used in the writing systems of ancient Assyria, Persia, and Anatolia.

daughter language
A language descended from a **protolanguage.**

dephonologization
Loss of a contrast and/or loss of a correlation. Compare **merger.**

desinence
Inflectional ending.

diachronic
Term used to characterize linguistic processes continuing through time.

diachronic correspondence
Relationship between two grammars such that the later grammar is derived from an earlier grammar by change in grammatical rules.

dialect borrowing
Adoption of linguistic features associated with speakers of a different form of the language of the recipient.

dissimilation
Process whereby a sound becomes less like another in its vicinity.

distant assimilation
Assimilation conditioned by a segment removed by at least one sound from the affected segment.

drag chain
A form of sound shift in which a sound changes to fill a gap in the sound system, and another sound begins to change in order to fill the gap created by the earlier change.

epenthesis
Insertion of vowels between consonants to facilitate pronunciation of articulatorily difficult consonant clusters. Also called **svarabhakti.**

etymological doublets
Two different words in one language having an identical etymological source.

etymology
Term referring to the study of the history of words.

false analogy
Term used (inappropriately) to characterize all types of linguistic change that find their motivation in morphological associations. See also **analogy, leveling.**

family tree hypothesis
Application of the hypothesis concerning the development of different species to the evolution of daughter languages from an ancestor language.

feeding order
Application of two rules, A and B, so that the output of A produces a form to which B will apply.

folk etymology
Reinterpretation of words whose surface morphology has become synchronically opaque using words or morphemes that are more familiar.

functional load.
See **functional yield.**

functional yield
Term referring to the frequency with which a phonemic distinction is used in a language to keep morphemes apart.

glottochronological constant
The percent of cognates assumed to remain in two languages after a thousand years of divergent development.

glottochronology
Method of **lexicostatistics** for determining degrees of relationship between languages, based on counting the number of cognates in a particular set of vocabulary items.

Grassmann's Law
Change of an aspirated stop into a plain (unaspirated) stop before another aspirated stop in the following syllable.

haplology
Loss of a syllable in a sequence of identical or nearly identical syllables.

hieroglyphic
Writing system consisting of picturelike symbols, where the symbols do not correspond in some direct and obvious fashion to the things to which they refer.

hypercorrection
Use of a historically unmotivated form for reasons of prestige.

ideographs
Symbols referring to broadly defined notions.

interference
Term referring to the effects of language contact between the two languages used by a bilingual speaker.

internal reconstruction
Procedure for inferring part of the history of a language from material available for a synchronic description of the language.

intimate borrowing
Transfer of linguistic features between two languages spoken within a single community.

isogloss
Line drawn on a map to surround the geographic area within which a linguistic feature may be found.

laryngeals
See **coéfficients sonantiques**.

lenition
Term used to refer to a sound change in Pre-Irish whereby voiceless stops become fricatives.

leveling
A historical process that reduces or completely eliminates allomorphy within a paradigm, usually achieved by generalization of one allomorphic variant.

lexical change
Changes in the meaning of words.

lexical diffusion
Assumption that sound change is phonetically abrupt, but lexically gradual; sound change does not affect all morphemes simultaneously, but spreads gradually through the lexicon.

lexicostatistics
Study of vocabulary statistically for historical inference. One method used is **glottochronology.**

linguistic affinity
Relationship between two languages in contact leading to the adoption of structural elements by one of the languages from the other when they correspond to its own tendencies of development.

linguistic alliance
See **Sprachbund.**

linguistic paleontology
Study of the meanings of words in a reconstructed language for the purpose of making social, cultural, and geographic inferences about the speech communities that used those languages.

loan translation
A type of cultural borrowing in which the model in the language of origin is translated, morpheme by morpheme, in the recipient language.

logographs
Symbols with a specific lexical referent.

markedness
The property that provides one member in a pair of oppositions with a distinguishing characteristic or 'mark'.

merger
Replacement of two or more contrastive segments by a single segment. Also called **coalescence**. Compare **dephonologization.**

metathesis
Reversal of the order of adjacent segments in specific lexical items, or in a class of forms that show specific sequences of segments.

morphological reanalysis
Reinterpretation of a sequence of morphemes either by reassignment of morpheme boundaries or by change in the identification of their function.

morphological reinterpretation
See **morphological reanalysis.**

morphologization
Development of new grammatical categories as a result of semantic differentiation of allomorphs.

murmur
A state of the glottis during which the vocal folds vibrate, while a considerable amount of air is escaping through the glottis.

Neogrammarian
Term used to refer to members of a group of linguistic scholars working in Leipzig in the second half of the nineteenth century.

Neogrammarian theory of sound change
See **regularity hypothesis.**

normal grade
The form of Indo-European roots in which the root vowel is *e*.

oblique cases
Cases other than the nominative (and accusative).

onomastics
The study of names.

overdifferentiation
Imposition of phonemic distinctions from a bilingual speaker's primary system to the sounds of his secondary system, where they are not required.

palatalization
An assimilatory sound change whereby a sound acquires a more palatal point of articulation.

paradigm
A set of inflected forms derived from the same root or stem.

paradigmatic leveling
A historical process that reduces or completely eliminates allomorphy under specific paradigmatic conditions.

paragoge
Development of word-final vowels.

parallel development
Change common to more than one language that is not due to inheritance from a common ancestor.

partial merger
The loss of one or more phonological distinctions in some specifiable phonetic environment.

philology
Science concerned with the analysis, interpretation, and restoration of archaic texts.

phone substitution
Transfer of phonetic realizations of identically defined phonemes from a bilingual speaker's primary language into his secondary language.

phonetic correspondence
The relationship between a sound at one point in the history of a language and the sound that is its direct descendent at any subsequent point in the history of that language.

phonetic process
Replacement of a sound or a sequence of sounds that presents some articulatory difficulty by another sound or sequence that lacks this difficulty.

phonic interference
The manner in which a speaker perceives and reproduces the sounds of his secondary language in terms of the system of his primary language.

phonographic writing system
System using symbols to represent sounds or sequences of sounds without regard to meaning.

phonological contrast
System of distinctive phonological oppositions.

phonological correlation
System of relationships that hold between features that characterize classes of sounds.

phonological restructuring
Any type of structural reorganization in the sound system of a language resulting in the loss of old contrasts, introduction of new contrasts, or realignment of elements within the system.

phonological reversion
A hypothetical situation involving reversal of phonological restructuring, such as reintroduction of a contrast after a complete merger in all and only those lexical contexts where the contrast existed before the merger.

phonologization
Change in the sound system of a language involving the development of conditioned allophones into separate phonemes as a result of loss of a conditioning factor. Compare **secondary split.**

pidgin
A language form arising from the need for communication among speakers of mutually unintelligible languages, characterized by highly simplified structure.

pidginization
Process whereby a pidgin is created using elements of some language as primary source.

prelanguage
Term used to refer to a period in the history of a language associated with a certain feature reconstructible through internal reconstruction.

primary split
Sound change affecting some allophones of a phoneme, which merge with another phoneme. No new phonemes are added to the sound system.

primary split from reassignment
Change in the phonological system involving phonological reinterpretation of unchanged segments.

progressive assimilation
Process whereby a sound acquires some features of a preceding sound.

prothetic vowel
Vowel developing in initial position in words originally beginning with a consonant.

protolanguage
Term used to refer to the earliest form of a language established by means of the comparative method of reconstruction.

push chain
A form of sound shift in which a change in one phoneme appears to cause a change in the same direction in another phoneme, so that merger may be avoided.

quantitative metathesis
Change in the ordering of distinctive length as a feature of adjacent segments—for example, a change of the type $\bar{V}\breve{V} > \breve{V}\bar{V}$.

reflex
A sound occupying a specific position in a particular morpheme, which appears to be a continuation of an earlier sound occupying the same position in the same morpheme at an earlier stage.

regrammatization
An alternation in the grammatical function of a morpheme.

regressive assimilation
Process whereby a sound acquires some of the features of a following sound. Compare **anticipatory assimilation.**

regularity hypothesis
Assumption that each sound of a given language will be changed similarly at every occurrence in like circumstances, if it is changed at all.

reinterpretation of distinctions
Process whereby a bilingual speaker distinguishes phonemes in his

secondary system by features that are concomitant or redundant in the secondary system but that are relevant in his primary system.

relatedness hypothesis
Hypothesis according to which obvious similarities between words belonging to different languages can be explained by assuming that the languages are descended from a common ancestor.

relexicalization
Changes in the phonological structure of morphemes.

rephonologization
Change involving reorganization in the system of correlations without any change in the manner of distinctive oppositions.

restructuring
Changes in the makeup of the phonological system.

rhotacism
A historical process involving the change of *s* or *z* to *r*, usually in intervocalic position.

rule inversion
Process whereby surface representations come to be reinterpreted as underlying representations, and forms consistent with the earlier underlying representations come to be derived by rule.

sandhi
Phonetic changes whose domain is more extensive than the individual word; loss, introduction, or alteration of a sound in the context of transition from one word to another.

secondary split
Sound change whereby conditioned allophones of a phoneme become independent phonemes as a result of a change in the environment that served to condition the occurrence of the allophones.

semantic paradigm
A set of words or morphemes belonging to a class that is defined by some close semantic relationship.

shared innovations
Innovations characterizing the period of common development of languages that later evolve into separate languages.

shortening
Abbreviated form replacing an older, longer version of the source word.

simplification (in syntactic change)
The tendency to change surface structures so as to make the semantic structure they represent more accessible to hearers.

sister languages
Related languages descended from a common ancestor.

sound change
Alterations in the phonetic shape of segments and suprasegmental features, which are the result of the operation of phonological processes.

sound correspondences
Sounds occurring in a particular place in a particular morpheme in cognate words found in related dialects or languages.

sound shift
Unconditioned sound changes affecting entire classes of sounds in a language.

split (in historical phonology)
Replacement of a single distinctive segment by two or more segments in different phonetic contexts. Compare **phonologization.**

split (in relation to the family tree hypothesis)
Start of divergent developments whereby a fairly homogeneous earlier stage is replaced by successor branches evolving into separate entities.

spontaneous sound change
See **unconditioned sound change.**

spoonerism
Also called **distant metathesis**, shift of order affecting segments in identical positions in different syllables or words.

Sprachbund
Linguistic alliance of a group of languages in contact, characterized by a development toward typological homogeneity regardless of genetic heterogeneity.

substratum
Former primary language of a group of speakers who have shifted to their formerly secondary language.

superstratum
Former primary language of a group of speakers who have entered a linguistic community and have been absorbed by that community, giving up their former primary language.

svarabhakti
See **epenthesis.**

syllabary
Writing system in which the symbols represent syllables.

synchronic
Term used to characterize linguistic processes and states describable at a given moment in time.

syncope
Loss of vowels within a word.

syncretism
Developments whereby grammatical distinctions are eliminated, either through phonetic change or through analogical processes.

syntactic analogy
Changes in syntax due to transfer of patterns on the basis of perceived formal relationships between pairs of sentence types.

syntagmatic
Term referring to relationships between elements in a linear sequence.

taboo word
Word that is avoided because of the sacred status of its referent or because of fear inspired by the referent.

thematic conjugation
Conjugation of a class of verbs in which a **thematic vowel** is introduced between the root and the desinence.

thematic vowel
Vowel introduced between the root and the desinence in certain classes of nouns and verbs.

umlaut
Change in the quality of a vowel due to the anticipated influence of a subsequent vowel.

unconditioned sound change
Sound change affecting every occurrence of a sound so that no conditioning factor can be identified.

underdifferentiation
Confusion of two sounds in a bilingual speaker's secondary system due to a lack of distinction bewteen these two sounds in his primary system.

vowel harmony
A type of progressive assimilation, in which the first vowel in a sequence constitutes the conditioning factor for subsequent vowels.

wave theory
Spread of linguistic innovations through language contact.

zero grade
The form of Indo-European roots in which the root vowel is absent. Compare **normal grade.**

BIBLIOGRAPHY

Andersen, H. (1973) "Abductive and deductive change" Language 49.4, 765-794.

Andersen, H. (1976) "Towards a Typology of Change: Analogy," in *Proceedings of the Second International Conference on Historical Linguistics*, Tucson, Arizona. W. Christie, ed. *Current Progress in Historical Linguistics*. North-Holland, Amsterdam.

Anttila, R. (1968) "The Relation between Internal Reconstruction and the Comparative Method," *Ural-Altaische Jahrbücher* 40, 159-173.

Anttila, R. (1974) *Analogy*, Department of General Linguistics, University of Helsinki.

Benveniste, E. (1968) "Mutations of Linguistic Categories," in W. P. Lehmann and Y. Malkiel, eds., *Directions for Historical Linguistics*, University of Texas Press, Austin, Texas, pp. 83-94.

Bergsland, K. and H. Vogt (1962) "On the Validity of Glottochronology," *Current Anthropology* 3, 115-153.

Bever, T., and D. T. Langendoen (1972) "The Interaction of Speech Perception and Grammatical Structure in the Evolution of Language," in R. Stockwell and R. Macaulay, eds., *Linguistic Change and Generative Theory*, Indiana University Press, Bloomington, Indiana, pp. 32-95.

Bloomfield, L. (1933) *Language*. Holt, Rinehart and Winston, New York.

Chafe, W. L. (1959) "Internal Reconstruction in Seneca," *Language* 35, 477-495.

Chen, M., and W. S.-Y. Wang (1975) "Sound Change: Actuation and Implementation," *Language* 51, 255-281.

Civ'jan, T. V. (1965) *Imja suščestvitel'noe v balkanskix jazykax*, Nauka, Moskva.

Cleator, P. E. (1959) *Lost Languages*. Mentor Books, New York.

Closs Traugott, E. (1965) "Diachronic Syntax and Generative Grammar," *Language* 41, 402-405.

Closs, E. (1969) "Toward a Grammar of Syntactic Change," *Lingua* 23, 1-27.

Clyne, M. (1972) *Perspectives on Language Contact*. The Hawthorn Press, Melbourne, Australia.

Clyne, M. (1975) *Forschungsbericht Sprachkontakt.* Scriptor-Verlag, Kronberg/Ts.

Diebold, A. R. (1976) "Contributions to the Indo-European Salmon Problem," in W. Christie, ed., *Current Progress in Historical Linguistics,* North-Holland, Amsterdam, pp. 341–388.

Friedrich, J. (1957) *Extinct Languages.* The Philosophical Library, New York.

Gelb, I. J. (1963) *A Study of Writing,* 2nd ed., University of Chicago Press, Chicago, Illinois.

Givón, T. (1971) "Historical Syntax and Synchronic Morphology," in *Proceedings of the 7th Regional Meeting of the Chicago Linguistic Society,* Chicago Linguistic Society, Chicago, Illinois, pp. 394–415.

Greenberg, J. (1966) "Some Universals of Grammar with Particular Reference to the Order of Meaningful Elements," in J. Greenberg, ed., *Universals of Language,* 2nd ed., MIT Press, Cambridge, Massachusetts, pp. 73–113.

Haas, M. R. (1966) "Historical Linguistics and Genetic Relationship," in *Current Trends in Linguistics,* vol. 3, Mouton, The Hague, pp. 113–153.

Hall, R. A. (1950) "The Reconstruction of Proto-Romance," *Language* 26, 6–27.

Hall, R. A. (1965) *Pidgin and Creole Languages,* Cornell University Press, Ithaca, New York.

Haugen, E. (1969) *The Norwegian Language in America: A Study in Bilingual Behavior,* 2nd ed., Indiana University Press, Bloomington, Indiana.

Hockett, C. F. (1948) "Implications of Bloomfield's Algonquian Studies," *Language* 24, 117–131.

Hockett, C. F. (1965) "Sound Change," *Language* 41, 185–215.

Hoenigswald, H. M. (1944) "Internal Reconstruction," *Studies in Linguistics* 2, 78–87.

Hoenigswald, H. M. (1946) "Sound Change and Linguistic Structure," *Language* 22, 138–143.

Hoenigswald, H. M. (1950) "The Principal Step in Comparative Grammar," *Language* 26, 357–364.

Hoenigswald, H. M. (1960) *Language Change and Linguistic Reconstruction,* University of Chicago Press, Chicago, Illinois.

Hoenigswald, H. M. (1963) "Criteria for Sub-grouping Languages," in H. Birnbaum and J. Puhvel, eds., *Ancient Indo-European Dialects,* University of California Press, Berkeley, California, pp. 1-12.

Hopper, P. J. (1973) "Glottalized and Murmured Occlusives in Indo-European," *Glossa* 7.2, 141-166.

Hymes, D. (1960) "Lexicostatistics So Far," *Current Anthropology* 1, 3-44.

Hymes, D. (1971) *Pidginization and Creolization of Languages.* University Press, Cambridge, England.

Jakobson, R. (1931) "Über die phonologischen Sprachbünde," *Travaux du Cercle Linguistique de Prague* 4, 234-240.

Jakobson, R. (1931) "Prinzipien der historischen Phonologie." *Travaux du Cercle Linguistique de Prague* 4, 277-287.

Jakobson, R. (1938) "Sur la theorie des affinités phonologiques entre les langues," in *Proceedings of the 4th International Congress of Linguists,* Copenhagen, pp. 48-59.

Jeffers, R. J. (1975) "On the Notion 'Explanation' in Historical Linguistics," in J. Anderson and C. Jones, eds., *Historical Linguistics,* North-Holland, Amsterdam, pp. 231-255.

Jeffers, R. J. (1976) "Syntactic Change and Syntactic Reconstruction," in W. Christie, ed., *Current Progress in Historical Linguistics,* North-Holland, Amsterdam, pp. 1-15.

Jeffers, R. J. (1976) 'Restructuring, Rephonologization and Reversion in Historical Phonology," in J. Fisiak, ed., *Recent Developments in Historical Phonology,* Mouton, The Hague.

Jeffers, R. J. (1977) "Morphological Reanalysis and Analogy: Two Case Histories from Latin and Greek," *Lingua* 41, 13-24.

King, R. D. (1969) *Historical Linguistics and Generative Grammar,* Prentice-Hall, Englewood Cliffs, New Jersey.

King, R. D. (1973) "Rule Insertion," *Language* 49, 551-576.

Kiparsky, P. (1968) "Linguistic Universals and Linguistic Change," in E. Bach and R. Harms, eds., *Universals in Linguistic Theory,* Holt, Rinehart and Winston, New York, pp. 171-204.

Klima, E. (1964) "Relations between Grammatical Systems," *Language* 40, 1-20.

Klima, E. (1965) *Studies in Diachronic Transformational Syntax,* unpublished dissertation, Harvard University, Cambridge, Massachusetts.

Kuryłowicz, J. (1945-1959) "La nature des proces dits 'analogiques', *Acta Linguistica* 5, 15-37.

Labov, W. (1972) *Sociolinguistic Patterns*, University of Pennsylvania Press, Philadelphia, Pennsylvania.

Lehiste, I. (1965) "A Poem in *Halbdeutsch* and Some Questions Concerning Substratum," *Word* 21, 55-69.

Lehmann, W. P. (1973) "A Structural Principle of Language and Its Implications," *Language* 49, 47-66.

Mallory, J. (1973) "A Short History of the Indo-European Problem," *Journal of Indo-European Studies* 1, 21-65.

Martinet, A. (1953) "Function, Structure, and Sound Change," *Word* 8, 1-32.

Meillet, A. (1970) *Le méthode comparative en linguistique historique*, H. Champion, Paris.

Parry, M. (1971) *The Making of Homeric Verse*, Clarendon Press, Oxford.

Paul, H. (1920) *Principien der Sprachgeschichte*, 5th ed., Niemeyer, Halle.

Postal, P. M. (1968) *Aspects of Phonological Theory*, Harper and Row, New York.

Sapir, E. (1921) *Language*, Harcourt, Brace and World, New York.

Schleicher, A. (1871) *Compendium der vergleichenden Grammatik der indogermanischen Sprachen*, Herman Böhlen, Weimar.

Schmidt, J. (1872) *Die Verwantschaftsverhältnisse der indogermanischen Sprachen.*

Stampe, D. (1969) "The Acquisition of Phonetic Representations," *CLS* 5, 443-454.

Stampe, D. (1973) *A Dissertation on Natural Phonology*, unpublished doctoral dissertation, University of Chicago.

Sturtevant, E. H. (1917) *Linguistic Change*, 1st ed., University of Chicago Press, Chicago, Illinois.

Swadesh, M. (1950) "Salish Internal Relationships," *IJAL* 16, 157-167.

Szemerenyi, O. (1962) "Principles of Etymological Research in the Indo-European Languages." 2. Fachtagung für indogermanische und allgemeine Sprachwissenschaft. *Innsbrucker Beiträge zur Kulturwissenschaft* 15, 175-212.

Vennemann, T. (1972) "Rule Inversion," *Lingua* 29, 209–242.

Vennemann, T. (1974) "An Explanation of Drift," in C. Li, ed., *Word Order and Word Order Change,* University of Texas Press, Austin, Texas, pp. 269–306.

Wang, W. S.-Y. (1969) "Competing Changes as a Cause of Residue," *Language* 45, 9–25.

Watkins, C. (1962) *Indo-European Origins of the Celtic Verb.* Dublin Institute for Advanced Study, Dublin.

Watkins, C. (1962) "Preliminaries to a Historical and Comparative Analysis of the Syntax of the Irish Verb," *Celtica* 5, 1–49.

Watkins, C. (1970) "A Further Remark on Lachmann's Law," *Harvard Studies in Classical Philology* 74, 55–66.

Weinreich, U. (1953) *Languages in Contact.* Linguistic Circle of New York, New York.

Weinreich, U., M. Herzog, and W. Labov (1968) "Empirical Foundations for a Theory of Language Change," in W. Lehmann and Y. Malkiel, eds., *Directions for Historical Linguistics,* University of Texas Press, Austin, Texas, pp. 95–188.

INDEX

Ablaut, 49, 72, 173
Absolute merger. *See* Merger
Absolute neutralization, 75, 117, 173
Accent, 9, 10, 21. *See also* Stress
 foreign, 139, 140, 142, 154
Actuation of sound change. *See* Phonological change
Adjacent assimilation. *See* Assimilation
Adstratum, 143, 144, 173
Afrikaans, 29
Agent, 117
Akkadian, 161, 163, 164
Albanian, 29, 145
Algonquian, 35
Alphabet. *See* Writing
Ambiguity in decipherment, 164–165
American structuralism,
 failings of, 81, 93
 and Neogrammarians, 91, 93
 and phonological change, 74–78, 85, 90–93, 98
Analogic creation, 60, 63–64, 72, 173
Analogic extension, 60–63, 71–72, 173. *See also* Analogy
Analogic leveling, 68
Analogic restoration, 69–70, 173. *See also* Phonological reversion
Analogy, 60–64, 65, 66–71, 96, 105, 115, 173, 177
 conditions for, 62, 66–68, 70–71
 false, 68, 177
 and syntactic change. *See* Syntactic change
Anaptyxis, 10, 11, 173
Anatolian, 29, 121
Ancient Egyptian. *See* Egyptian

Ancient Greek. *See* Greek
Ancient Indic. *See* Indic
Andersen, Henning, 73, 105
Anderson, J. M., 73
Anticipatory assimilation. *See* Assimilation, regressive
Anttila, Raimo, 54, 73
Aorist
 in Armenian, 63–64, 72
 in Greek, 69–70
Aphesis (Aphaeresis), 10, 11, 174
Apocope, 10, 11, 174
Arabic, 11
Armenian, 7, 11, 29, 63–64, 72, 135
Arrow, 1–2
Articulatory target, 92–93
 and expectancy distribution, 92
 and frequency maximum, 92
Aśoka, 169
Assamese, 32
Assimilation, 3–6, 12, 21, 174, 181
 adjacent, 5–6, 173
 complete, 4–5
 distant, 5–6, 22, 177
 partial, 4–5
 progressive, 5, 24, 183, 187
 regressive, 5, 24, 90, 183
Asterisk, 20, 114
Attic Greek. *See* Greek
Avestan, 29

Bach, Emmon, 105
Back formation, 65–66, 174
Backing, 6, 13
Balkanisms, 145–146, 174
Backing, 6, 13
Balkanisms, 145–146, 174
Baltic, 29, 79
 Proto-Baltic, 71
Baltic German, 155–158

Balto-Finnic, 21, 28
Proto-Balto-Finnic, 21, 23, 24
Balto-Slavic, 29
Bengali, 27–29, 30–32
Benveniste, Emile, 73
Bergsland, Knut, 135, 136, 137
Bever, Thomas, 113–114, 124
Bilingualism, 163, 164
  and linguistic change, 138,
    139–140, 141–142, 150, 155,
    178, 180, 181, 183, 187
Bleeding order. *See* Rule order
Blend. *See* Word formation
Bloomfield, Leonard, 16, 35, 73,
    90–93, 102, 105, 137, 146,
    158, 170
Borrowing, 33–35, 138, 165, 174
  cultural, 147–150, 176, 179
  dialect, 147, 153–155, 176
  and integration into borrowing
    language, 147–150, 152
  intimate, 147, 149, 150–153,
    178
  and lexical change, 134, 135,
    141, 145, 151, 154
  loan words, 11, 47, 136, 141,
    142, 144, 148, 149, 151, 152,
    153
  and sound change, 11, 34, 47,
    148
  and structural change, 146,
    147, 148–149
Brahmins, 170
Brand names, 128
Breton, 29
Brugmann, Karl, 68–69, 89
Brythonic, 29
Bulgarian, 29, 145–146
Byelorussian, 29, 79–80, 144

Canonical shape, 47, 104, 157
Cartouche, 163. *See also*
  Writing
Case markers, 9, 37–38, 43–44,
    61–63, 70, 71–73, 107, 115,
    117, 145. *See also* Des-
    inence; Grammatical
    categories; Oblique cases
  in Halbdeutsch, 157, 158
Catalan, 29
Cave drawings, 160
Celtic, 29, 46, 79, 123, 125, 142,
    155
  Early, 30
  Pre-, 58
Centralization, 13
Chafe, Wallace, 37, 39, 54
Chen, Matthew, 103, 105
Cheremis (Mari), 28
Chinese, 104, 140, 161
Christie, William, 73, 125
Civ'jan, Tat'jana Vladimirovna,
    146
Classical Latin. *See* Latin
Classical Sanskrit. *See* Sanskrit
Cleator, P. E., 170
Closs Traugott, Elizabeth, 124
Clyne, Michael, 159
Coalescence. *See* Merger
Code switching, 149, 174
Coéfficients sonantiques, 48–50,
    52, 174
Cognates, 17, 30–31, 33, 34, 35,
    37, 45, 51, 121, 122–123, 175
  and glottochronolgy *(See* Glot-
    tochronology)
  and lexical change *(See* Lex-
    ical change)
  and sound change 17,18, 19,
    21, 22, 27, 41, 50, 57, 91,
    119–120
Coinage. *See* Word formation
Common innovations. *See*
  Innovations
Common language, 52, 175. *See
  also* Family tree hypothesis
Common Slavic. *See* Slavic
Comparative morphology, and
  syntactic reconstruction, 120

Comparative reconstruction,
   17–35, 50, 132–133, 175, 183.
   See also Reconstruction
   and borrowing, 33–35, 138
   relation to internal recon-
      struction, 37, 41, 51–53
   and syntactic change *(See*
      Reconstruction)
Compensatory lengthening, 12,
   50, 175
Complete merger. *See* Absolute
   neutralization
Conditioned sound change. *See*
   Sound change
Consonant mutations. *See*
   Mutations
Contamination, 57–59
   leveling within semantic par-
      adigms, 57, 175, 184
Context. *See* Lexical change,
   Linguistic change
Context-free sound change. *See*
   Sound change, uncondi-
   tioned
Context-sensitive sound change.
   See Sound change, condi-
   tioned
Cornish, 29
Correspondences, 71, 122, 123,
   131
   diachronic, 98, 176
   one-to-one, 120, 160
   phonetic, 1–2, 8, 9, 12, 89–90,
      98, 181
   and the regularity hypothesis,
      17
   sound, 17–26, 34, 49, 185
Correspondence set, 18, 21, 22,
   23, 33, 52, 120
Counter-bleeding order. *See*
   Rule order
Counter-feeding order. *See* Rule
   order
Creole, 158, 176
Cultural borrowing. *See*
   Borrowing

Cuneiform. *See* Writing
Czech, 29, 144, 151

Dacorumanian, 152
Danish, 29, 144
Daughter language, 18, 27, 31,
   34, 124, 175, 176, 177. *See
   also* Family tree hypothesis
Deletion of segments, 3, 10–12,
   13, 76, 117,
   historical cases of, 13, 22, 23,
      33, 38, 39–40, 43–44, 49–50,
      51, 55, 58, 65, 70, 72, 99,
      100–101, 121
Dephonologization, 79–80, 176,
   180
   and merger, 79, 176
de Saussure, Ferdinand, 48–50,
   52, 54, 174
Desinence, 61, 64–65, 176, 186.
   See also Case markers
Diachronic correspondence. *See*
   Correspondences
Diachrony, 1, 98, 119, 139, 158,
   160, 167, 168, 170, 176
Dialect borrowing. *See* Bor-
   rowing
Dialectology, 103, 154. *See also*
   Borrowing, dialect
Diebold, A. Richard, 132
Diphthongization, 14, 15, 99–
   100, 151–152
Dissimilation, 3, 6, 176
Distant assimilation. *See*
   Assimilation
Doric Greek. *See* Greek
Drag chain, 94–95, 177
   in Provençal, 95
Dutch, 29

Early Celtic. *See* Celtic
Ease of articulation. *See*
   Phonological change
East Germanic. *See* Germanic
East Slavic. *See* Slavic

Egill Skallagrimsson, 168
Egyptian, 162
  Ancient, 161, 163
  Neo-, 163
Ejectives, 26
  in Indo-European, 26
Elamite, 163, 164
English, 29, 34, 42, 77, 94, 108
  borrowing, 147–148, 149, 150–
    151, 152, 153, 154–155
  change in morphological sys-
    tem of, 57–58, 65, 66, 70–71
  language contact in, 139, 140,
    141, 142, 143–144
  lexical change in, 126, 127,
    128, 129–130, 131, 132, 135,
    136
  Middle, 10, 12, 57, 65, 128
  Old, 4, 12, 57, 78, 100–101,
    115, 127, 129, 149, 151
  sound change in, 4, 5, 6, 7, 8,
    10, 11, 12, 13–14
  syntactic change in, 111, 113–
    115, 117
Environment, 41–42, 139. *See
  also* Reconstruction
  of sound change, 20, 21, 22–
    23, 75, 90, 175, 184
Epenthesis, 10, 11, 173, 177
Ergativity, 124
Erza, 28
Eskimo, 135
Estonian, 22–25, 28, 155–158,
  168
Etymological doublets, 153, 177
Etymology, 131, 132, 153, 177.
  See also Borrowing, and
  lexical change
Evidence for historical linguis-
  tics, 160–170. *See also*
  Reconstruction, and writing
Excrescence, 11–12

False analogy. *See* Analogy

Family tree hypothesis, 27–32,
  33, 52, 135
  node, 31, 52, 177
  prelanguage. *See* Prelanguage
  protolanguage. *See* Proto-
    language
Features, 138, 139, 144, 147
  distinctive, 79, 80, 81, 82
  phonetic, 19, 26, 43, 74
  phonological, 3, 51
  prosodic, 14
  and sound change, 1, 98, 173,
    182
  typological, 143
Feeding order. *See* Rule order
Finnish, 22–25, 28, 99, 140, 144,
  151–152, 168
  Proto-Finnic, 28
Finno-Ugric, 21, 28
Fisiak, Jacek, 87
Fleeting vowels. *See* Russian
Flemish, 29
Folk etymology, 66, 177
Folk songs. *See* Writing
Formulaic texts, 163–164, 168.
  See also Writing
French, 4, 29
  borrowing, 147, 148, 149–150
  Middle, 128, 153
  Norman, 143–144, 150–151, 152
  Old, 12, 65
  sound change in, 6, 10, 12
Friedrich, Johannes, 171
Frisian, 29
Fronting, 2, 6, 13, 22, 77
Functional load. *See* Functional
  yield
Functional yield, 94, 177
Futhark. *See* Runes

Gaelic. *See* Irish
Garden path sentence, 115
Gelb, I. J., 171
Gender, 140, 141, 150, 157

Generative grammar. *See also*
    Grammar change; Syntactic
    change
  failings of, 85–86, 98
  and innovations. *See* Inno-
    vations
  and language acquisition in
    linguistic change, 96–98
  and Neogrammarians, 96
  and phonological change, 74,
    81, 82–87, 96–101
  and structuralism, 96, 98
Genetic relationship, 33, 86,
    134, 143, 158
  subgrouping, 31–32
Georgian, 135
German, 6, 29, 34, 37–39, 42,
    64–65, 66, 70, 71, 83–84,
    128, 135, 136, 140, 141, 143,
    144, 148, 155
  Low, 29
  Middle High, 65, 71, 78, 83
  Old High, 65, 75, 77–78
  Standard, 29
Germanic, 9, 20, 29, 33, 34, 42,
    63, 123, 126, 127, 132, 143,
    151, 152, 157, 167
  East, 29
  First Germanic Consonant
    Shift, 13–14, 58, 77
  North, 29, 33, 167
  phonological change in, 75, 77–
    78, 83
  Pre-, 51, 57
  Proto-, 33, 42, 51–52, 57, 75,
    153
  West, 29, 33
Germanic consonant shift, 13,
    58, 77
Gilliéron, Jules, 103
Givón, Talmy, 125
Glossary, 173–187
Glottalization, 26
Glottochronological constant,
    134, 135, 136, 137, 178

Glottochronology,
  and cognates, 133–137, 178
  and core vocabulary, 134
  and lexicostatistics, 133–137,
    178, 179
  problems of, 134–136
  and semantic field, 134
  and time depth, 133, 134, 136,
    137
Goidelic, 29
Gothic, 9, 20–21, 29, 33, 34, 42,
    60, 62–63, 167
Grammar change, 66, 67, 71–73,
    96–98, 117, 120. *See also*
    Linguistic change; Gener-
    ative grammar
Grammatical categories, 57, 71–
    73, 104, 117, 123, 124, 140,
    148, 180. *See also* Case
    markers
Grassmann's Law, 6, 178
Great English vowel shift, 13–
    14, 126.
Greek, 10, 29, 34, 49, 50, 51,
    57, 58, 60, 73, 77, 127, 132,
    145–146, 147, 152, 162, 167
  Ancient, 30, 55–56, 57, 69–70,
    72, 126, 132, 149, 163, 169
  reconstruction in, 17–20, 38–
    40, 49
  sound change in, 2, 4, 6, 7, 8–
    9
  Attic, 7, 9, 81–82
  Doric, 55–56, 68
  Homeric, 55–56, 169
  Pre-, 2, 8, 51, 55, 81–82
  sound change in, 2, 4, 5, 6, 7,
    9, 47
Greenberg, Joseph, 118, 125

Haas, Mary, 35
Halbdeutsch, 155–158, 159
Hall, Robert A., Jr., 35, 159
Hanti. *See* Ostyak
Haplology, 11, 178

Harms, Robert, 105
Haugen, Einar, 159
Hellenic, 29
Herzog, Marvin, 106
Hiberno-English, 154–155, 157
Hieroglyphics. *See* Writing
Hindi, 4, 29, 30–32, 34–35, 140
Hirt, Hermann, 107–108
Hittite, 29, 50, 64, 121–122, 123, 161, 164
Hockett, Charles, 35, 92–93, 98, 105
Hoenigswald, Henry, 20, 35, 54, 75, 87
Homer, 9, 38, 55, 169
Homeric Greek. *See* Greek
Hopper, Paul, 26, 36
Hrozný, Bedrich, 50
Hungarian (Magyar), 28, 140, 144, 145, 152
Hymes, Dell, 137, 158, 159
Hypercorrections, 178

Icelandic, 29, 135, 144
Ideographs. *See* Writing
Idioms, 129–130, 153
Iliad, 169
Indic, 20, 27, 29, 30, 49, 170
  Ancient, 169
  Middle, 35, 169
  Old, 27, 35
  Pre-, 59, 84
  Proto-Eastern, 32
Indo-European, 27, 30, 34, 35, 36, 46, 51, 54, 64, 67, 72, 73, 79, 109, 110, 121, 124, 125, 127, 131–132, 137, 169
  fable *(See* Reconstruction)
  laryngeals, 48–50, 174
  passives, 116, 123
  reconstruction, 17–18, 19, 77, 107
  roots, 180, 187
Indo-Iranian, 29
Infinitival complement, in Sanskrit. *See* Sanskrit

Innovations, 19, 27, 30, 32–33, 55, 57, 58, 62, 65–66, 67, 71–72, 116, 123, 130, 174. *See also* Wave theory
  and generative grammar, 83, 85, 86, 96–97, 98, 111, 112
  and language contact, 32, 143, 145, 151, 152, 153–154, 187
  shared, 31–33, 53, 145, 184
Inscriptions. *See* Writing
Insertion of segments, 3, 10–12, 13, 22
Interference, 178
  morphosyntactic, 140–141
  phonic, 139–140, 181
  overdifferentiation of, 139, 140, 180
  phone substitution of, 140, 141, 181
  reinterpretation of, 139–140, 141, 154, 157, 183
  underdifferentiation of, 139, 140, 157, 187
Internal reconstruction, 37–53, 120, 123–124, 178, 182. *See also* Comparative reconstruction
  later obscuring of, 39–46, 55
  and paradigmatic alternations, 37–41, 43–45, 56, 48–50, 52, 55–57, 120 (*See also* Phonological change)
  and structural inconsistency, 46–50
Intimate borrowing. *See* Borrowing
Intrusive segments. *See* Insertion of segments
Iranian, 29, 48, 79
Irish, 6, 13, 125, 155
  Gaelic, 29, 154–155
  Old, 13, 30, 43–46, 47, 58, 121–122
  Pre-, 121–122
Isogloss, 154, 178
Italian, 4, 5, 6, 15, 29, 145
Italic, 29

Jakobson, Roman, 78, 87, 93, 143, 159
Jeffers, Robert, 73, 87, 125
Jones, Charles, 73

Karelian (Olonets), 28
King, Robert, 82, 87, 96, 97
Kiparsky, Paul, 96, 99, 105
Klima, Edward, 97, 111, 125
Komi. *See* Zyrian
Kurdish, 29
Kuryłowicz, Jerzy, 50, 70, 73

Labialization, 4, 43
Labov, William, 102–103, 105, 106, 153
Lachmann's Law, 73
Langendoen, D. Terence, 113–114, 124
Language acquisition, 96–98, 101. *See also* Linguistic change
and imperfect learning, 98
and optimal grammar, 97
Language acquisition device, 97
Language contact, 185, 187
and borrowing, 11. *See also* Borrowing
and creolization, 158
and interference (*See* Interference)
and linguistic change, 11, 27, 135, 138–158, 174
primary language, 139, 140, 141, 142, 173, 176, 180, 181, 183, 186, 187
secondary language, 138, 139, 140, 141, 142, 155, 180, 181, 183, 186, 187
Language convergence, 143, 144, 146
Language family, 18, 27, 31, 86, 88. *See also* Family tree hypothesis
and glottochronology, 133
Lapp, 28

Laryngeals. *See* Coéfficients sonantiques
Latin, 29, 34, 35, 47, 58, 60, 65, 66–68, 73, 76, 77, 86, 126, 127, 132, 135, 141
borrowing, 147, 148, 149, 152, 153
Classical, 76
Old, 76
Pre-, 67, 76
sound change, 4, 6, 10, 11, 12, 14–15
Vulgar, 12, 15
Latvian, 29, 71–72, 80, 136, 144
Lehiste, Ilse, 155, 159
Lehmann, Winfred P., 73, 106, 125
Lenition, 121–122, 179
Leveling, 55–57, 69, 96, 105, 121, 175, 177, 178, 181
analogic (*See* Analogic leveling)
in grammatical categories, 57
and phonological change, 56–57, 70, 78, 83, 84
and rule loss, 83
and rule reordering, 84
Lexical change, 63, 126–137, 179
and cognates, 127, 132–133
and etymology (*See* Etymology)
and extension of referents or contexts, 127–128, 129, 130
and glottochronology (*See* Glottochronology)
and language contact, 141, 154
and reduction of referents and contexts, 127, 128, 129, 136, 152–153
and replacements of referents, 126–127
and taboo words (*See* Taboo words)
and word formation (*See* Word formation)

Lexical diffusion
  and phonological change, 100,
    103–104, 179
  and tone, 104
Lexicostatistics. *See* Glotto-
    chronology
Linear A, 164
Linguistic affinity, 143–144, 179
Linguistic alliance. *See*
    Sprachbund
Linguistic change, 7, 68, 160,
    170.
  and analogy (*See* Analogy)
  and child language acquisition,
    96–98
  and complexity, 101
  and context, 19–20, 57, 64, 67–
    68, 78, 90, 91, 102–103, 126
  and ease of articulation (*See*
    Phonological change)
  explanation of, 69, 88, 102–103
  as grammar change (*See* Gram-
    mar change)
  and language contact (*See*
    Language contact)
  and morphological systems,
    55–73, 103–105, 107, 152,
    153
Linguistic paleontology, 131–
    132, 179
Linguistic universals. *See*
    universals
Lithuanina, 29, 71, 144
Livonian, 21–25, 28
Loan translation, 149, 179
Loan word. *See* Borrowing
Logographs. *See* Writing
Lowering, 6, 13
Low German. *See* German
Lude, 28

Macaulay, Ronald, 124
Macedonian, 145–146
Magyar. *See* Hungarian
Malkiel, Yakov, 73, 106

Mallory, James, 137
Mansi, 28
Mari. *See* Cheremis
Markedness. *See* Rule reorder-
    ing
Martinet, André, 93–95, 96, 105
Mayan, 164
Medio-passive, in Old Persian,
    165
Meillet, Antoine, 36
Merger, 33, 41–42, 51, 59, 180,
    183
  absolute, 41–42, 47, 75, 76, 85,
    173, 182
  partial, 42–44, 75, 181
  and phonological change, 75–
    76, 77–78, 79, 81, 85, 86, 94
Metaphorical extension, 128,
    130. *See also* Lexical change
Metathesis, 6–9, 11, 72, 180
  distant (*See* Spoonerism)
  quantitative, 9, 183
Meter, 168
Middle English. *See* English
Middle French. *See* French
Middle High German. *See*
    German
Middle Indic. *See* Indic
Middle Persian. *See* Persian
Minimal pairs, 15, 144, 151
Mixed language. *See* Writing
Mnemonic devices, 160
Modern Standard Russian. *See*
    Russian
Moksha, 28
Monophthongization, 23
Mordwin, 28
Morphological change. *See*
    Linguistic change; Recon-
    struction
Morphological reanalysis, 64–
    69, 122, 180
Morphological reinterpretation.
    See Morphological reanalysis

Morphological system, and linguistic change. *See* Linguistic change
Morphologization, 71–73, 180
Morphophonemic change, 48–50, 53, 58–59, 85, 104–105. *See also* Reconstruction
Morphosyntactic interference. *See* Interference
Münter, Friedrich, 163
Murmur, 6, 26, 180
Mutations, in Irish, 13, 44

Natural phonology
failings of, 102
and language change, 101–102
Neo-Egyptian. *See* Egyptian
Neogrammarians, 69, 180
and regularity hypothesis, 89
and theories of phonological change, 69, 89–90, 91, 93, 96, 102
Neogrammarian theory of sound change. *See* Regularity hypothesis
Neutralization. *See* Absolute neutralization
Nominal complement, in Sanskrit. *See* Sanskrit
Normal grade. *See* Root
Norman French. *See* French
Norse, 34
Old, 34, 167–168
North Germanic. *See* Germanic
North Kashubian. *See* Slovincian
Norwegian, 29, 144, 159
Number, 140

Oblique cases, 70, 180
Odyssey, 169
Old Church Slavic, 5, 7, 17–20, 29, 53, 56, 60–62, 167
Old English. *See* English
Old French. *See* French

Old High German. *See* German
Old Indic. *See* Indic
Old Irish. *See* Irish
Old Latin. *See* Latin
Old Norse. *See* Norse
Old Persian. *See* Persian
Old Prussian. *See* Prussian
Old Russian. *See* Russian
Old Spanish. *See* Spanish
Olonets. *See* Karelian
Onomastics. *See* Writing
Optative, in Armenian, 63
Oriya, 29, 32
Orthography, 10. *See also* Writing
Osthoff, Hermann, 89
Ostyak, 28
Overdifferentiation. *See* Interference
Oxford English Dictionary, 130

Palatalization, 4, 8–9, 24, 43–44, 53, 56, 181
in Slavic, 43–44, 53, 56, 79–80
Panini, 110
Paradigm, 37, 38, 39, 40, 43–44, 55–57, 59, 60–61, 64, 68, 78, 83, 104, 120–121, 173, 179, 181
Paradigmatic leveling. *See* Leveling
Paragoge, 11, 181
Parallel development, 33, 53, 123, 181
Parent language, 19, 20, 21, 27, 51, 52, 55, 62, 63, 116, 122, 123, 124. *See also* Family tree hypothesis
Parry, Milman, 171
Partial merger. *See* Merger
Pashto, 29
Passive
in Greek,
in Sanskrit, 116–117
Paul, Hermann, 69, 90, 105

Pehlevi. *See* Persian, Middle
Perceptual strategy. *See* Syntactic change
Periphrastic, 123
Permian, 28
Permian-Finnic, 28
Persian, 29
  Middle, 164
  Old, 72, 163–166
Philology. *See* Writing
Phoneme, 94, 139, 140, 144, 148, 151, 154, 156, 182, 183. *See also* Phonological change; Sound change
Phonemic inventory, 51, 75, 76, 77, 86, 88
  gaps in, 47, 94–95
Phone substitution. *See* Interference
Phonetic change. *See* Sound change
Phonetic correspondence. *See* Correspondence
Phonetic process. *See* Process
Phonic interference. *See* Interference
Phonographic writing system. *See* Writing
Phonological change, 14, 75–87, 151–152. *See also* Sound change
  actuation of, 92–93, 102, 103, 173
  and American structuralism. *See* American structuralism
  and ease of articulation, 10, 11, 90, 93, 96
  explanation in, 2, 85–86, 88–105
  and generative grammar. *See* Generative grammar
  and lexical diffusion *(See* Lexical diffusion)
  and morphological change *(See* Linguistic change)
  and Neogrammarians *(See* Neogrammarian)
  and paradigmatic leveling *(See* Leveling)
  and Prague school structuralism *(See* Prague school)
  social motivations for, 102–103, 138
  sporadic, 89, 91
  and syntactic change *(See* Syntactic change)
  transition problems in, 103
Phonological contrast, 27, 75, 76, 79, 82, 85, 180. *See also* Phonological restructuring
Phonological correlation, 79, 80, 81, 82, 94, 156, 176, 182, 184
Phonological restructuring, 15, 19, 74, 76, 78, 86, 182, 183
  and split, 27, 30–31, 75, 85
Phonological reversion, 56, 76, 182
Phonological system, 14–15, 20, 21, 25, 27, 30, 31–32, 51, 53, 74, 75, 78, 79, 81, 82, 83, 85, 92, 101, 112, 119, 148, 182
  natural (symmetrical), 47, 94
Phonological universals. *See* Universals
Phonologization, 79, 80, 182, 185
  and split, 79, 80, 85, 182
Pidgin, 158, 176, 182
Pidginization, 182
Pleonastic formations, 70–71, 145
Poetry. *See* Writing
Polish, 29
Portuguese, 4, 29
Postal, Paul, 96, 98, 105
Prague school
  failings of, 81–82, 95
  and phonological change, 74, 78–82, 85, 93–95, 101
Pre-Celtic. *See* Celtic

Pre-Germanic. *See* Germanic
Pre-Greek. *See* Greek
Pre-Indic. *See* Indic
Pre-Irish. *See* Irish
Prelanguage, 51–52, 182
Pre-Latin. *See* Latin
Pre-Slavic. *See* Slavic
Primary language. *See* Language contact
Primary split. *See* Split
Processes, 4, 8, 12, 44, 84, 96, 121, 138
  natural, 101–102
  phonetic, 1–2, 12, 13, 181
  phonological, 1, 8, 168, 185
Progressive assimilation. *See* Assimilation
Proper names, 127
Prothetic vowel, 7, 10–11, 183
Proto-Baltic. *See* Baltic
Proto-Balto-Finnic. *See* Balto-Finnic
Proto-Eastern Indic. *See* Indic
Proto-Finnic. *See* Finnish
Proto-Germanic. *See* Germanic
Proto-Indo-European, 18, 20, 21, 29, 33, 42, 55, 56, 57–58, 62, 64, 65, 67, 69, 72, 75, 80–81, 110, 127, 131, 132
  homeland, 131–132
  reconstruction in, 25–26, 30, 34, 48, 49, 107, 121, 122
Protolanguage, 17, 21, 25, 51–53, 124, 175, 183
Proto-Oriya-Assamese-Bengali. *See* Indic, Proto-Eastern
Proto-Romance. *See* Romance
Prototype, 21, 49, 52
Provençal, 29, 95
Prussian, Old, 29
Push chain, 94–95, 183

Quantitative metathesis. *See* Metathesis

Quantity, 9, 12, 14–15, 21–22, 27, 50, 83–84, 140, 144, 146, 156–157
Quisling, Vidkun, 127

Radicals. *See* Writing, logographic
Raising, 6, 9, 13, 14
Reconstruction, 12, 51–53, 55, 88, 91, 120, 127, 131, 148, 152, 160, 179
  comparative (*See* Comparative reconstruction)
  internal (*See* Internal reconstruction)
  and mixed-language texts, 170
  phonetic reality of reconstructed forms, 19, 25–26, 42–45
  of substratum language, 155–158
  syntactic, 107–110, 119–124
    and comparative method, 119–122, 124
    difficulties in, 119, 120, 121, 122
    Indo-European fable, 107–108
  and writing (*See* Writing)
Reduplication, 6
Reflex, 18, 19, 20, 21, 32, 34, 51, 58, 62, 63, 65, 67, 81, 104, 121, 123, 131, 132, 183
Regrammatization, 64–65, 183
Regressive assimilation. *See* Assimilation
Regularity hypothesis, 17, 19, 183
Reinterpretation
  of distinctions (*See* Interference)
  of meaning, 129
Relatedness hypothesis, 17, 184
Relative clause, 118, 121
  in English, 113–115, 155
Relexicalization, 86–87, 184

Reordering of segments, 3, 6–9.
  See also Metathesis
Rephonologization, 80–82, 184
Restructuring. *See* Phonological
  restructuring
Retroflexion, 12
Rhotacism, 67, 76, 86, 184
Rig Veda, 109–110, 170
Romance languages, 4, 15, 136,
  142, 145, 152
  Proto-, 35
Romany, 29
Root, 12, 77, 126, 186, 187. *See
  also* Verbal root
  in Indo-European, 48–50, 67,
    127, 174, 180
  normal grade, 48–50, 174, 180,
    187
  zero grade, 48–50, 187
Rosetta Stone. *See* Writing
Rounding, 13
Rule addition, 82–83, 85, 96, 97,
  98
  and phonetic split, 85
Rule change, 82–86, 96, 111–113
  conditions determining, 98, 99
  constraints on, 98–99
Rule inversion, 82, 84, 85, 184
Rule loss, 82, 83, 84, 85
Rule order, 99
  bleeding, 99, 101, 174, 176
  counter-bleeding, 99, 175, 176
  counter-feeding, 99, 100, 101,
    176
  feeding, 99, 100, 101, 176, 177
Rule reordering, 82
  explanation of, 99–101
  and markedness, 99–100, 112,
    179
  and paradigmatic leveling, 100
  in phonology, 82, 83, 84, 85
  in syntax, 111–112
Rumanian, 4, 29, 145, 152
Runes, 167
Russian, 29, 34, 53, 58, 70, 79,
  127, 132, 140, 144, 149–150

imperative, 56, 69
Modern Standard, 56
Old, 56

Salish, 137
Samoyed, 28
Sandhi, 13, 44, 184
Sanskrit, 10, 34, 35, 48–50, 58,
  59, 72, 77–78, 80, 84–85,
  107, 109–110, 116–177, 132
  Classical, 40–42, 59
  reconstruction, 17–20, 20–21,
    121–122, 123
  sound change, 4, 5, 6, 7, 12
  Vedic, 121–122, 170
Sapir, Edward, 16, 73, 125, 159
Sarvelian (Finnish), 99–100
Scandinavian, 42, 149, 151, 153
Schleicher, August, 27, 31, 107
Schmidt, Johannes, 32
Schuchardt, Hugo, 103
Scots Gaelic, 29
Scribal errors. *See* Writing
Secondary language. *See*
  Language contact
Secondary split. *See* Split
Semantic change. *See* Lexical
  change
Semantic context. *See* Syntactic
  change
Semantic field. *See* Glotto-
  chronology
Semantic paradigm. *See* Con-
  tamination
Semantic structure. *See*
  Underlying structure
Semitic languages, 162
Seneca, 54
Serbo-Croatian, 29, 141, 145–
  146
Shared innovations. *See* Inno-
  vations
Shortening. *See* Word formation
Simplification, 59, 68, 78, 157
  in syntactic change, 78, 112–
    113, 185

Sister language, 18, 19, 34, 52,
    122, 185. *See also* Family
    tree hypothesis
Slavic, 5, 7–8, 29, 34, 53, 58,
    61–62, 79, 80–81, 127, 132,
    143, 145, 152, 167
  Common, 52
  East, 29
  Palatalization, 5, 53, 56
  Pre-, 7, 53, 56, 81
  South, 29, 146
  West, 29, 144
Slovak, 29
  Western, 144
  Eastern, 144
Slovene, 29, 146
Slovincian (North Kashubian),
    144
Social motivation for sound
    change. *See* Phonological
    change
Sociolinguistics, 102, 154, 158
Sound addition. *See* Insertion of
    segments
Sound change, 1–15, 17, 18, 22–
    23, 24, 27, 31, 32, 34, 56, 57,
    59, 60, 62, 63, 67, 69, 71, 75,
    78, 83, 86, 103, 107, 119–
    120, 121, 122, 135, 136, 148,
    149, 185. *See also* Phono-
    logical change
  classification of, 3–15
  conditioned, 3–13, 53, 78, 82–
    83, 90, 101, 104–105, 175
  and conditioning factors, 3, 5,
    6, 9, 13, 15, 41, 43–45, 90,
    96, 187
  and explanation of change, 2,
    90, 93
  reconstruction of, 37–40, 47,
    51, 53
  domain, 13
  as phonological change, 14, 74,
    92, 98
  unconditioned, 3, 13, 80, 90,
    93, 94, 185, 187

Sound correspondences. *See*
    Correspondences
Sound loss. *See* Deletion of
    segments
Sound shifts, 13–14, 93, 94–95,
    177, 183, 185
South Slavic. *See* Slavic
Spanish, 4, 5, 11, 29, 139, 140
  Old, 11
Spirantization, 45
Split, 41, 135
  and conditioned merger, 76
  and the family tree hypothesis,
    27, 30–31, 86, 185
  and historical phonology, 75,
    76–78, 79, 85, 185
  and phonological restructuring
    (*See* Phonological restruc-
    turing)
  primary, 76–77, 81, 182
    from reassignment, 77, 183
  secondary, 77–78, 80, 85, 86,
    182, 184
Spontaneous sound change. *See*
    Sound change, uncondi-
    tioned
Spooner, William, 7
Spoonerism, 7, 185
Sprachbund, 143, 144, 146, 174,
    185
Stampe, David, 101, 105
Standard German. *See* German
Stockwell, Robert, 124
Stress, 3, 10, 14, 15. *See also*
    Accent
Structuralist school, 86, 91–96,
    126. *See also.* American
    structuralism; Prague school
Sturtevant, Edgar, 137
Subgrouping. *See* Genetic
    relationship
Subjunctive, in Armenian, 63–
    64
Substratum, 142, 146, 154, 186
  in Ireland, 142, 154–155

reconstruction of (*See* Reconstruction)
Sumerian, 161, 164, 165
Superstratum, 142, 146, 186
in France, 142
Suprasegmentals, 1, 3, 14–15, 185
Surface structure, 82, 96, 101, 109, 110, 111, 112–113, 115, 118, 124, 184, 185. *See also* Grammar change
Svarabhakti. *See* Epenthesis
Swadesh, Morris, 133–134, 135, 137
Swedish, 29, 144
Syllabary. *See* Writing
Synchrony, 1, 31, 51, 60, 63, 66, 88, 91–92, 109, 124, 160, 177, 178, 186
alternation in synchronic system, 37–40, 41–44, 46, 53, 78, 82
and sound change, 1, 3, 83, 84–85, 152.
Syncope, 10, 11, 12, 70, 186
Syncretism, 71–72, 186
Syntactic analogy, 115–118, 186
Syntactic change, 107–124. *See also* Reconstruction
and analogy, 115–118
explanation of, 104, 112, 119
and perceptual strategies, 112–115
and phonological change, 13, 117, 119
renewed interest in, 108
and semantic context, 107, 117
and sentence patterns, 107, 115–117, 120, 122–123
and typology, 118–119, 124
and word order, 118–119, 123, 124
Syntagmatic relationship, 3, 44, 90, 186
Szemerenyi, Oswald, 137

Taboo words, 132, 135, 186
Tautosyllabic, 71, 77
Taxonomy
and sound change, 2, 3, 86
structuralist, 81, 85, 92
Thai, 139
Thematic conjugation, 67, 186
Thematic vowel, 67, 186
Thracian, 152
Time depth. *See* Glottochronology
Tocharian, 29
A, 29
B, 29
Tone, 14, 144, 146
and lexical diffusion (*See* Lexical diffusion)
Topicalization, in Hiberno-English, 154–155
Transformational rules, 109
changes in 111–112
Transitivity, 116, 124
Turkish, 140–141, 145, 152
Typology, 69, 74, 75, 88, 93, 173. *See also* Syntactic change

Udmurt. *See* Votyak
Ugric, 28
Ukrainian, 29, 79–80, 144
Umlaut, 6, 22, 24, 33, 65, 70, 77, 83, 100–101, 126, 168, 187
Underdifferentiation. *See* Interference
Underlying structure, 82, 96, 109, 110, 112, 113, 184. *See also* Generative grammar
Universals. *See also* Word order
linguistic, and syntactic change, 108–109, 118–119
phonological, 25–26, 47
Uralic, 27, 28
Urdu, 29

Variables in change, 102–103
Varro, 60
Vedic Sanskrit. *See* Sanskrit
Velarization, 140
Vennemann, Theo, 82, 87, 105, 117, 125
Veps, 28
Verbal root, 67, 69–70, 110, 116, 157
Verbal stem, 67, 69, 110
Verner, Karl, 90
Vogt, Hans, 135, 137
Vogul (Mansi), 28
Volga-Finnic, 28
Vote, 28
Votyak (Udmurt), 28
Vowel harmony, 6, 187
Vowel loss. *See* Deletion of segments
Vowel quality, 5–6, 8, 15, 22, 23–24, 43, 49–50, 78, 95, 99, 140
Vulgar Latin. *See* Latin

Wang, William S-Y. 103, 105, 106
Watkins, Calvert, 73, 121, 125
Wave theory, 32
and linguistic innovation, 32–33, 143, 187
Weakening, of intervocalic consonants, 45
Weinreich, Uriel, 106, 139, 143, 159
Welsh, 29
West Germanic. *See* Germanic
West Slavic. *See* Slavic
Word formation, 130–131
blending, 130–131, 174
coinage, 130–131, 175
shortening, 130–131, 185
Word order, 118–119, 124, 141. *See also* Syntactic change

implicational universals of, 118
in Indo-European, 123
Writing, 160
alphabet, 161, 163
as evidence for reconstruction of linguistic change, 20, 69, 123, 133, 155–158, 160–170
deciphering extinct systems, 162–165
cuneiform, 163–165, 176
hieroglyphics, 162–163, 164, 178
Linear A, 164
onomastics, 166, 180
parallel texts, 167
problems of, 162, 164–165
Rosetta Stone, 163
scribal error, 166–167
and translations, 167
development of, 160–162
ideographic, 161, 162, 178
inscriptions, 126, 165–166, 167, 169
logographic, 161, 164, 179
logosyllabary, 163
materials, 166
and oral tradition, 167–170
folk songs, 168
mixed language, 169–170
poetry, 55, 155, 167–169, 170
problems of, 169–170
Vedic hymns, 109–110, 170
and philology, 123, 162, 165–170, 181
phonographic, 161, 162, 164, 165, 182
syllabary, 161, 162, 163, 164, 165, 186

Yiddish, 29, 83, 143

Zero grade. *See* Root
Zyrian (Komi), 28